Talk for Writing

Andrew Hammond

CONTENTS

PRINCIPLES OF MIND'S EYE TALK FOR WRITING

This resource recognises the importance of Talk for Writing and the need to embed teacher and pupil talk in all stages of the teaching sequence.

The **stimuli** (sounds and images) along with the **introduction** are particularly supportive of whole class teaching and learning, whilst the **writing activities** and **photocopymasters** are particularly suited to supporting guided and independent writing.

This resource also offers support for the hardest parts of writing and turns pupil 'talk for writing' into *the* writing.

HOW TO USE MIND'S EYE TALK FOR WRITING

Preparation and planning

Use the chart on p3 to check out which unit fits with your planning requirements in terms of the core learning in literacy from the Primary Framework.

Use the chart on p64 to check out the range of genres, text types and cross-curricular coverage of your chosen unit.

Read the Teacher's Notes to make selections and personalise for the needs of your class as appropriate.

Select the writing activity you want to focus on or decide which groups will work on which writing outcomes.

Photocopy the student activity sheet as appropriate (photocopymaster).

Bring up the unit image or sound file and 'hide' using the hide and reveal tool on your interactive whiteboard.

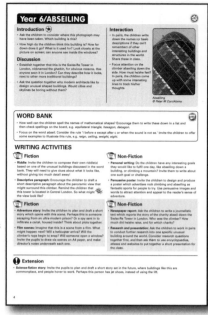

 Use the *Mind's Eye Writing Year 6* CD.

 Ask children to consider an image in their mind's eye.

The hardest parts of writing:	Mind's Eye Talk for Writing Suggested lesson sequence:
Having the ideas and enough ideas to sustain the writing.	**Introduction** 1. Capture interest with image or sound. 2. Talk about the image or sound. 3. Activate prior knowledge from pupils. 4. Encourage an open-ended eliciting and development of response. **Discussion** Use 'teacher talk' prompts to stimulate group or class discussion. **Interaction** Ideas for setting up a range of oral paired activities and small discussion groups to capture the ideas and rehearse these.
Using good vocabulary and achieving expression.	**Word Bank** Topic-related vocabulary and specific spelling rules and conventions that will complement and develop the pupils' knowledge and expertise. Practising these ideas and rehearsing them ensures that pupils are not hindered by a lack of the basics when they begin writing.
Shaping the whole and using appropriate and varied sentences.	**Writing Activities** For each unit, eight writing activities are suggested; two short activities for both fiction and non-fiction and two longer activities for both fiction and non-fiction. In each case teacher prompts are provided to ensure that the teaching sequence for writing is maintained: 1. Familiarisation with the genre/text type 2. Capturing ideas/oral rehearsal in line with the task 3. Teacher demonstration 4. Teacher scribing/supported writing/guided writing.
Independent writing	The outcome of each writing activity along with the use of the photocopymaster provided supports the pupil in independent writing.

CREATIVE THINKING (YEAR 6)

The introductory sessions, word bank activities and writing activities in *Mind's Eye: Talk for Writing (Year 6)* all help to raise standards in writing through the promotion of creative thinking. In the publication *Excellence and Enjoyment: Learning and teaching in the primary years* (DfES 0518-2004G) creative thinking is identified as a key aspect of learning. It involves the children in:

• generating imaginative ideas
• discovering and making connections

• exploring and experimenting
• asking questions
• trying alternative or different approaches
• looking at things from other points of view
• making connections and seeing relationships
• reflecting critically on ideas, actions and outcomes.

These strategies are incorporated into each unit in *Mind's Eye: Talk for Writing (Year 6)*.

CORE LEARNING FOR LITERACY – STRANDS AND OBJECTIVES (YEAR 6)
From Primary Framework for Literacy and Mathematics 02011-2006BOK-EN

Core learning in literacy strands for Year 6 (numbers correspond to paragraphs/points within each strand)

Mind's Eye Images Unit	1 Speaking	2 Listening and responding	3 Group discussion and interaction	4 Drama	6 Word structure and spelling	7 Understanding and interpreting texts	8 Engaging with and responding to texts	9 Creating and shaping texts	10 Text structure and organisation	11 Sentence structure and punctuation	12 Presentation
ABSEILING	1, 3	2	2		1, 2	2, 4, 5		2, 3, 5	1, 2	2	
BALL AND CHAIN	1, 2, 3	1, 4	1		1	2, 4		1, 2, 5	2	2	2
CANDLE	1, 3	2, 3		1	1	2, 4	3	2, 4, 5	1, 2	1, 2	
COASTLINE	3	2		1, 2		2, 3		1, 2, 3	1, 2	2	1, 2
COMPASS	2	1, 2	2		1	1, 3	3	2, 3	1	1, 2	2
DERELICT BUILDING	3	1, 3			1, 2	4		2, 3, 4, 5	1, 2	2	2
DOORS	3	3, 4	2	1	1, 2	3		2, 3	1, 2	2	1, 2
HANDS	1, 3	2, 3	2		1	3, 5		2, 3, 5	1, 2	2	
HIPPOS	3	1, 3		1, 2	1, 2	2, 5		1, 2, 5	1, 2	2	2
HOUSES OF PARLIAMENT	1, 2, 3	1, 2, 3	1, 2	1, 2, 3	1, 2	2, 5	3	2, 4, 5	2	1, 2	1, 2
JET FIGHTER	3	1, 2	1, 2	1	2	2		1, 2, 3	2	2	
KEYHOLE	3	2			1, 2	2, 3, 4		2, 3, 5	1, 2	1, 2	1
MISTY HARBOUR	1	1, 3	2		2	2, 3		2, 3, 5	2	2	
NEPALESE TOWN	3	1, 2			1	2, 3, 4	3	2, 5	1, 2	1, 2	1
OLD PHOTOGRAPH	2, 3	2, 4	1, 2	1, 2	2	2, 4	3	4, 5	2	1, 2	
RIDERS	2, 3	1, 2	2	1	2	2, 3		2, 3, 4	2	1, 2	
ROBOWOMAN	1, 2, 3	1		1	1, 2	3, 4		3, 4, 5	1, 2	1, 2	2
ROLLER COASTER	3	1, 2		1	2	3		1, 2, 3, 5	1, 2	2	2
ROOFTOPS	3	1	2		1, 2	2, 4		1, 2, 4	2	2	2
TREKKING	3	2, 4		1	1, 2	2, 3		2, 3, 5	1, 2	1, 2	2

Core learning in literacy strands for Year 6 (numbers correspond to paragraphs/points within each strand)

Mind's Eye Sounds Unit	1 Speaking	2 Listening and responding	3 Group discussion and interaction	4 Drama	6 Word structure and spelling	7 Understanding and interpreting texts	8 Engaging with and responding to texts	9 Creating and shaping texts	10 Text structure and organisation	11 Sentence structure and punctuation	12 Presentation
ALARM CLOCK	3	2, 3			1, 2	3, 4		1, 2, 5	1, 2	2	
BABY CRYING	3	2	2		2	2, 3, 4		2, 3, 5	1, 2	1, 2	1
CICADAS AT NIGHT	1, 3	1, 2	1, 2	1	1, 2	2, 3, 5		2, 3, 4, 5	1, 2	1, 2	2
DRUM ROLL	3	1			2	4		2, 3, 5	2	2	
GORILLA	2, 3	1, 2	1, 2	1, 2, 3	1, 2	2		1, 2, 3	1, 2	1, 2	2
GUNFIRE	1, 2, 3	1	1, 2	1	1, 2	2, 5		2, 3, 4, 5	1, 2	2	1
POLICE SIREN	3	2, 3	1	1	1, 2	4, 5		1, 2, 5	2	2	
SCUBA DIVING	1, 3	1, 2	2	1, 3	1, 2	1, 5		2, 3, 5	1, 2	1, 2	2
TENNIS CROWD	2, 3	1, 2	1, 2	1, 3	2	4, 5		1, 2, 3	1, 2	2	1
WATER DRIPPING	1, 3	1, 3, 4	1	1	1, 2	4, 5		2, 3, 5	1, 2	1, 2	

Introduction

- Ask the children to consider where this photograph may have been taken. Which building is this?

- How high do the children think this building is? How far down does it go? What is it used for? Look closely at the picture on screen; can anyone see inside the windows?

Discussion

- Establish together that this is the Swiss-Re Tower in London, nicknamed the gherkin, for obvious reasons. Has anyone seen it in London? Can they describe how it looks, next to other more traditional buildings?

- Ask the question together why modern architects like to design unusual shaped buildings. Would cities and skylines be boring without them?

Interaction

- In pairs, the children write down the names (or basic descriptions if they can't remember) of other interesting buildings and structures in the world. Share these in class.

- Focus attention on the climber abseiling down the side. How must he/she feel? In pairs, the children come up with some interesting lines to track his/her thoughts.

Abseiling
© Peter M Corr/Alamy

WORD BANK

- How well can the children spell the names of mathematical shapes? Encourage them to write these down in a list and then check spellings on the board, e.g. *equilateral triangle, hexagon, decagon*.

- Focus on the word *abseil*. Consider the rule 'i before e except after c or when the sound is not ee.' Invite the children to offer some examples to illustrate this rule, e.g. *reign, ceiling, weight, eight*.

WRITING ACTIVITIES

Fiction

- **Riddle:** Invite the children to compose their own riddle(s) based on one of the unusual buildings discussed in the word bank. They will need to give clues about what it looks like, without giving too much detail away!

- **Descriptive paragraph:** Encourage the children to draft a short descriptive paragraph about the panoramic view that might surround this climber. Remind the children that this tower is located in Central London. So what might the view look like?

Non-Fiction

- **Personal writing:** Do the children have any interesting goals they would like to fulfil one day, like abseiling down a building, or climbing a mountain? Invite them to write about one such goal or challenge.

- **Persuasive poster:** Invite the children to design and produce a poster which advertises rock climbing and abseiling as fantastic sports for people to try. Use persuasive images and words to attract attention and appeal to the reader's sense of adventure.

Fiction

- **Adventure story:** Invite the children to plan and draft a short story which opens with this scene. Perhaps this is someone escaping from an ultra-modern prison? Or a spy sent in to infiltrate a cartel, housed inside? Think about plots together.

- **Film scenes:** Imagine that this is a scene from a film. What might happen next? Will a helicopter arrive? Will the climber's rope begin to snap? Will someone open a window? Invite the pupils to draw six scenes on A4 paper, and make director's notes underneath each one.

Non-Fiction

- **Newspaper report:** Ask the children to write a journalistic text which reports the story of the charity abseil down the Swiss-Re Tower in London. Who was the climber? How much did he/she raise, and for which charity?

- **Research and presentation:** Ask the children to work in pairs to conduct further research into one specific unusual building around the world. Consider research questions together first, and then ask them to use encyclopaedias, atlases and websites to put together a short presentation for the class.

❗ Extension

- **Science-fiction story:** Invite the pupils to plan and draft a short story set in the future, where buildings like this are commonplace, and people hover to work. Perhaps this person has jet shoes, instead of using the lift.

SIR NORMAN FOSTER

The Swiss-Re Tower (or Gherkin) in London was designed by the famous architect, Sir Norman Foster.

Find out more about the life and work of Foster. Use encyclopaedias, magazines, newspaper archives and websites to find out all you can.

Make notes as you go along. Then share your findings with the class.

_____

_____

_____

_____

_____

_____

_____

_____

_____

_____

_____

_____

_____

_____

Note: Extra sensitivity may be required if any of the children are known to have family members in prison.

Introduction

- Ask the children to share the first words and phrases that enter their head when they see this picture – anything will do! Record these words on the board and discuss them.
- Consider the colours of this image. How do they contribute to the impact it leaves on the viewer?

Discussion

- Consider together where this may have been taken, i.e. where is it meant to be? Share ideas in class (e.g. in prison, torture chamber, museum, etc.).
- How do the children *feel* when they see this picture? List some adjectives – e.g. f*rightened, unsettled, curious, uncomfortable.*

Interaction

- In small discussion groups, the children discuss the purpose of imprisonment. Is it to protect the rest of society or to remove freedom as a punishment, or both? Are there better ways of dealing with criminals? Share feedback in a plenary session.
- How would the children feel if they were locked up in this way? Invite volunteers to sit in the 'hot seat' and answer questions in the role of someone who has worn these shackles for years.

Ball and Chain
© Larry Lilac/Alamy

WORD BANK

- Thinking back to the earlier brainstorm, encourage the children to compile their own word bank of adjectives to describe the way this picture makes them feel.
- Invite the pupils to make two lists of descriptive words: one to describe the feeling of being imprisoned, and the other to record words to describe being free, e.g. *worthless/special.*

WRITING ACTIVITIES

Fiction

- **Paired words:** Explain that the words *ball* and *chain* go together, and can be used in many different ways and contexts. What other words go together? The pupils list paired words and share them in class, e.g. *salt and pepper, strawberries and cream, peace and quiet, crime and punishment*, etc.
- **Descriptive poem:** Using the descriptive words from the word bank, the pupils write a poem to describe the feeling of being imprisoned, and then the feeling of being freed. Share in class.

Fiction

- **Short story:** Invite the children to plan and draft a short story in which a prisoner is dreaming about life outside. What do they miss about the outside world? Do they dream about being rescued? Try to avoid the standard 'and then I woke up' ending!
- **Descriptive paragraph:** Look again at the image. Invite the children to imagine that the door of a dark cell has just been opened to find the prisoner has escaped. Describe the scene in detail from the prison officer's point of view, as he/she slowly opens the door.

Non-Fiction

- **Diary:** Ask the children to write a fictional recount excerpt in which they describe the first day they are thrown into a prison cell, for a crime they did not commit.
- **Persuasive poster:** Invite the children to design and produce a poster which persuades young readers to stay out of trouble. They may use incentives, like the success and happiness that come from good behaviour and hard work, and/or warnings showing what happens when criminals get caught.

Non-Fiction

- **Information text:** Invite the children to draft a short information text displaying – through words and pictures – the forms of imprisonment and torture used dungeons in olden times, e.g. stocks, thumb screws, rack, etc. Use a range of supervised internet visits and library research.
- **Debate speech:** Ask the children to draft a short speech proposing or opposing the following motion: *This House believes that a life sentence should mean life, and convicted murderers should remain in prison until they die.*

Extension

- **Fantasy story:** Invite the children to write a short story in which they are sent away to a prison in space, where all the criminals of the world are locked up, well away from the people on Earth. But in their case, they did not commit the crime of which they stand accused.

Name _____   Date _____

What does the dark mean to you? How do you feel in the dark?

What about the light? How do you feel when a light is switched on and you can see all around you?

Which do you prefer? Write down some abstract nouns we might associate with being in the light and dark.

In the Light	In the Dark
happiness	loneliness
honesty	secrecy

Introduction

- Ask the children to share the first words and phrases that enter their head when they see this picture – anything will do! Record these words on the board and discuss them.

- Discuss the parts of the candle – i.e. *wick, flame, wax,* etc. Discuss how a candle works.

Discussion

- Consider together what we often associate candles with – the occasion and the setting, e.g. *church ceremonies, romantic meals,* etc. List these on the board.

- What did people do before we had electric lights? And before gas lamps? What must life have been like when everywhere was lit by candlelight? Share thoughts and opinions.

Interaction

- In small groups, the children play out a short scene which must involve a candle in some way, e.g. romantic meal, birthday party, etc.

- Circle game: introduce a game in which the children all hold out a pretend candle, tiptoe together into a huddle and then say softly 'Ladies and Gentlemen, the King has gone to bed'. Then they blow out their candle. Repeat this several times. If anyone laughs, giggles, or smirks, they have to sit out!

Candle © Ian Simpson/Alamy

WORD BANK

- Ask the children, individually or in groups, to write down some interesting abstract nouns to describe the feelings associated with the image of the candle, e.g. *romance, peace, faith, life.* Share these in class and invite the children to talk about the words they have chosen.

- See how many adjectives the children can think of that are associated with light. Record these in word banks and share in class, e.g. *bright, blinding, illuminating, fresh, happy, exciting, warm.*

WRITING ACTIVITIES

Fiction

- **Acrostic poem:** Invite the children to compose an acrostic poem using the word *candle* as the key word down the left hand side. Each line can give more information about the candle, or describe the peaceful atmosphere that candles can bring.

- **Descriptive paragraph:** Ask the children to draft a short descriptive piece in which they describe one particular setting – taken from earlier discussions – in which a candle helps to create an atmosphere.

Fiction

- **Historical story:** Invite the children to plan and draft a short story set in a historical setting, where candles and fires were the only form of lighting, e.g. in a medieval castle.

- **Mystery story:** Ask the pupils to plan and draft a short story which begins with a scene in which the lights are suddenly extinguished somewhere and a crime is committed. How will the truth be revealed? What clues are there in the room?

Non-Fiction

- **Personal writing:** Invite the children to write a short paragraph in response to the following question: *What does a candle mean to you?* Share responses in a plenary session.

- **Information poster:** Invite the children to design and produce a poster which informs readers how to save electricity in the home by remembering to switch off the lights before leaving a room, and avoiding using them if it is already light in a room.

Non-Fiction

- **Chronological report:** Invite the children to research how lights have evolved in our society through the ages, from fire, to candles, gas lights and electric bulbs and torches. Then encourage them to display this information in a chronological report, using diagrams, sketches, annotations and dates.

- **Explanation text:** Ask the children to design and produce a short explanation text which explains to readers how a candle works, through labelled diagrams and paragraphs. Refer back to the earlier discussion about the various parts of the candle and their functions.

Extension

- **Thoughtful writing:** Remind the children that a flame (i.e. fire) is one of the most precious things to Man. What other precious, important things can they think of that are around them (visible or invisible)? Encourage them to write each one down, with a few sentences to explain why they have chosen it. (E.g. *trees, gold, love, friendship.*)

CHARACTER PROFILE

Look again at the image. Imagine that this candle is being carried by someone, as they wander up to their bedroom in a great house or castle, many years ago.

What does this person look like? Can you picture him/her in your mind's eye?

Write a description of this character, including his/her appearance, movement and personality.

_____

_____

_____

_____

_____

_____

_____

_____

_____

_____

Introduction

- Where do the children think this image was taken? In the British Isles or beyond?

- Explore this scene further: is there land on the horizon too, or clouds and sea? Consider together what the rest of the scene might look like – to the left, right and behind the camera.

Discussion

- Discuss together whether this would be a good place to holiday by the coast. What sort of holiday would it be? E.g. a beach holiday? A walking holiday?

- Elicit the children's knowledge and experience of coastal walks. Why are they dangerous? What should they do to keep safe in such places? (E.g. *don't walk too close to the edge, be accompanied*.)

Interaction

- In groups of four, the children role-play a scene in which two of them are out walking along this particular stretch of coastline, when they meet another pair of walkers. They begin a conversation, discussing where they are going, whether they are locals or tourists, how often they have been, etc.

- Invite the children to think of their favourite place – or natural view – in the British Isles. Then encourage volunteers to come to the front and describe it as vividly as they can for the class.

Coastline © Niall Benvie/Alamy

WORD BANK

- Ask the children to make two lists: one for adjectives to describe the ocean, in all its different states and moods, and the other for the rocky coast. Share interesting words in a plenary.

- Consider together how such a view makes us feel. Why do so many of us find coastal walks peaceful and calming? Encourage the children to articulate how they feel when they see this picture.

WRITING ACTIVITIES

Fiction

- **Descriptive poem:** Invite the children to compose a descriptive poem in which they describe a smuggler's cave down by the sea, surrounded by treacherous rocks, but bursting with treasures from afar.

- **Descriptive paragraph:** Ask the children to draft a short descriptive piece in which they describe their favourite natural view in the British Isles, as mentioned in the earlier class discussion.

Fiction

- **Sea adventure:** Encourage the children to plan and draft a short story in which they are sailing on board a galleon many years ago, bound for new waters, never explored before. They stumble across a new island, or cliffs and green fields. Where is this place? Who inhabits its? What happens next?

- **Mystery story:** Ask the children to plan and draft another short story, this time about a group of children who stumble across a smuggler's cave down by the sea, while on a school field trip. It still contains some treasure…

Non-Fiction

- **Personal writing:** Invite the children to write a short paragraph in which they attempt to explain why so many people are attracted to coastal walks and view points. What is it about the sea that attracts us so much? Encourage the children to share their own explanations for this on paper.

- **Advertisement:** The children imagine they are working for a coastal tourist board. Their task is to design a poster that persuades people to come to the rural coast for their holidays. Discuss together why tourists should visit this kind of coastline rather than beaches and traditional seaside towns.

Non-Fiction

- **Safety poster:** Refer back to the discussion on how to keep safe when walking along coastal paths. Then invite the children to draft a poster which gives younger walkers important advice on how to keep safe when walking by the coast. Discuss in class and then share work when it is finished.

- **Personal recount:** Where is the furthest the children have travelled to in the British Isles? Why did they go there? What happened? Get out maps and atlases to help them decide which is the furthest point they have visited. Then encourage them to write a short recount of their trip.

Extension

- **Research and presentation:** Ask the children to find out more about our coastline. How long is the entire perimeter of our coast? How many seaside towns do we have along it? How many beaches? Using the Internet and atlases and books, the children find out lots of information and then present it to the class.

Name _____ Date _____

SKULL ISLAND

Skull Island is a legendary place, feared by sailors throughout the world for its treacherous rocks, its crumbling cliffs and the strange and mysterious places that lurk deep within the island, like *Death Valley, Whispering Woods* and the famous *Castle of Doom*.

Draw a map of this fictional island, showing these, and other features of the island.

Introduction

- Ask the children to share their initial responses to this image. Brainstorm the first words that enter the children's heads (e.g. *map and compass, orienteering, expedition,* etc.).

- Look closely at the image; can anyone work out where it is? Can they make out any names of places or features? Is the main town 'Chaumont'? Where is that?

Discussion

- Discuss together the function of compasses. When and where are they used? Elicit the children's knowledge and experiences of map-and-compass work.

- Discuss together other ways in which people might be able to navigate their way around, without the use of a compass, e.g. *position of the sun, the stars at night time.*

Interaction

- In pairs, the children think about where this particular compass might have been. What sort of expeditions has it been used in? Share ideas and thoughts in class, each pair reporting back in a plenary session.

- Nowadays, many cars are fitted with satellite navigation systems. Is this a good thing? What happens when the system breaks down (which it probably will!)? Will we remember how to use a map? Are we relying too much on computer technology? Discuss these issues in groups/class.

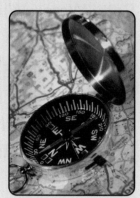

Compass © Steve Allen/Alamy

WORD BANK

- Ask the children to make a list of all the features they can think of that might be found on an Ordnance Survey map, like the one in the image. Share and check spelling, e.g. *roads, railway lines, churches, public houses,* etc.

- Consider together the use of imperative verbs in directions, e.g. *take, turn, pass, continue.* Ask the children to write down as many as they can and then share them in class.

WRITING ACTIVITIES

 ## Fiction

- **Character study:** Ask the children to write a character profile in which they describe a fictional traveller who might use this map and compass – is it an explorer, a soldier or perhaps a scout?

- **Geographical poem:** Invite the children to draft a poem, containing four stanzas. Each one describes a land that lies far to the north, south, east or west of this country. E.g. Greenland, Australia, Malaysia, USA.

 ## Fiction

- **Adventure story:** Invite the children to plan and draft a short story in which the central character joins an expedition to some far flung place, that requires careful map reading to reach it, e.g. deep in the jungle, North Pole, Everest, Sahara, etc. What happens along the way?

- **Descriptive poem:** Ask the children to write a descriptive poem about a journey that stretches from a cold place to a very warm place, (e.g. a flight to Malaysia). Focus especially on the contrasting feel of the climate, the landscape and the plants and wildlife in each different place.

 ## Non-Fiction

- **Directions:** Ask the children to each write a short set of directions to lead from their own house to school. These may include references to road names and numbers, landmarks and other notable features along the way. (Consider together the imperative verbs in the word banks.)

- **Route map:** Ask the children to convert the directions above into a route map – a sketch of the journey, featuring the same names and features, with arrows to show the direction to be taken.

 ## Non-Fiction

- **Recount:** Ask the pupils to draft a recount of a journey they have taken recently, that involved a road atlas or map and compass. It may have been a car journey to see a relative, or a holiday, etc. Encourage them to think about the stages of the journey, the stops, the long hauls and the scenery along the way. Encourage them to keep to a chronological order.

- **Factual description:** Consider together what is to the north, south, east and west of your school. Refer to a local map or road atlas for details. Then encourage the children to write a description of what lies in each direction, thinking about roads, towns and landmarks.

 ## Extension

- **Chronological report:** Ask the children to conduct some research into how people navigated their way around before the advent of modern technology. Using the Internet and encyclopaedias, the pupils find evidence and then present it in a written chronological report or timeline.

NEVER EAT SALTY WATER!

Read the title of this worksheet again: Never Eat Salty Water. What do you notice about the first letter of each word?

They read: N, E, S, W – North, East, South and West! This is a mnemonic, a clever way of remembering the order of the compass points, starting at the top and working clockwise around in a circle.

Can you think of your own mnemonics for North, East, South and West? Have a go at writing some interesting ones below.

N _____

E _____

S _____

W_____

N _____

E _____

S _____

W_____

N _____

E _____

S _____

W_____

N _____

E _____

S _____

W_____

Introduction

- Ask the children to share their initial responses to this image. Brainstorm the first words that enter the children's heads.

- Look again at the image. Consider together where this may have been taken. What sort of building might it be?

Discussion

- Discuss together how this image makes the children feel. What sort of emotions does it conjure up, and why?

- Consider together the mood of this picture, focusing particularly on the black and white. How different might it be if it were in colour? How different would the atmosphere and mood be if the bricks were in red and the windows were in cream? Would it be less austere/unsettling?

Interaction

- In pairs, the children think of stories that this building could tell. What happened to it? Why is it derelict? What was it like once? A thriving factory perhaps, or a family home?

- Encourage the children to 'see' the rest of this building, and the surrounding area. Ask for volunteers to describe it for the class, so that others can share in their imagination.

Derelict Building © TF1 /Alamy

WORD BANK

- Ask the children to make a list of words to describe their feelings upon seeing this derelict building, e.g. *fear, sympathy, pity, curiosity, interest, abandonment, loneliness*, etc. Share these in a plenary.

- Consider together what this building might look like inside. Then invite the children to make two lists of adjectives, to describe the interior and the exterior of this building.

WRITING ACTIVITIES

Fiction

- **Descriptive writing:** Ask the pupils to draft a short piece of descriptive prose in which they make use of all the words in their word banks to describe this building in detail: inside and outside, appearance and atmosphere.

- **Short descriptive poem:** Ask the children to focus on a different building – real or fictional – which has also been abandoned in this way. Then invite them to write a short poem about it, focusing particularly on personifying the building in some way – giving it emotions and thoughts.

Non-Fiction

- **Sales particulars:** Ask the children to draft the opening paragraph of some sales particulars for this property, were it to be put on the market by property agents. Discuss together how agents try to present buildings in a favourable light, e.g. 'with great potential for improvement!'

- **Synonyms:** Encourage the children to use a thesaurus to record down different synonyms for *derelict*. Share these in class and discuss the effects of each one. Are some more dramatic than others?

Fiction

- **Long descriptive poem:** Get hold of a copy of Walter de la Mare's *The Listeners*. After reading it to the children, invite them to write a similar kind of poem, in which they describe the atmosphere inside this derelict building, it having stood empty for many years, until someone comes along....

- **Mystery story:** Invite the children to plan and draft a short story about a derelict old building that hides some interesting secrets, which are discovered by some local children who go exploring where they shouldn't.

Non-Fiction

- **Letter of complaint:** Suggest to the children that they are actually local residents, living in full view of this building, which is a local council property, now disused and dilapidated. Ask them to write a letter of complaint each, to the council, asking them to do something about it.

- **Newspaper report:** Invite the class to reflect on what was found hidden in this building, in the mystery stories they wrote (above). Then ask them to write a local newspaper article, reporting the find. Encourage them to present reactions and comments from the finders, local neighbours and the owner(s) of the property.

Extension

- **Personal writing:** Invite the children to reflect again on what might have happened to this building. Then ask them to write down their theories in a short paragraph or two, stating what the building once was, and why it fell into this state of disrepair. Encourage the pupils to talk about their own ideas.

Name _____ Date _____

The following words might all be used to describe a building. Some of them would be more appropriate for a derelict building. Others you might use to describe a more cheerful place.

Sort them out into two columns, one for each type of building. You might need to use a dictionary!

dilapidated   happy   unloved

noisy

lively   colourful   drab

inhospitable   friendly   austere

charming

gloomy   cherished   vacant

A Derelict House	A Family Home

Introduction

- Ask the children to share their initial responses to this image. Brainstorm the first words that enter the children's heads. Is it a new building or an old one? How can we tell?

- Look again at the image. Consider together where this may have been taken. Is this an entrance into a building or an exit out of one? How can we tell?

Discussion

- Elicit the children's knowledge and experience of doors of this kind. Has anyone seen some like it before? Where? Share experiences and make some guesses about where this is set.

- Discuss together why closed doors often seem inviting to us. Is it because of our curiosity to peer through, or perhaps even stop and eavesdrop?

Interaction

- Working pairs, invite the children to play '20 questions' in which one partner thinks of something (or someone) who is hiding behind the door. The other must guess who it is by asking up to 20 questions, the answers to which may only be 'yes' or 'no'.

- In pairs again, this time the pupils think up some interesting, science-fictional ideas and story plots based around these doors. What mysterious place, or laboratory, might they lead to?

Doors
© Image Source/Alamy

WORD BANK

- Introduce/revisit antonyms by using the terms *open* and *closed*. Encourage the children to think of more pairs of antonyms and then share them in class, checking spelling each time. Can they think of antonyms relating to this image? (E.g. *light/dark, in/out; white/black; welcome/unwelcome*.)

- Invite the pupils to make a list of interesting adjectives to describe these doors, and the fictional laboratory or other unusual place that may lie beyond them (referring back to discussion above).

WRITING ACTIVITIES

Short task | Fiction

- **Riddles:** Challenge the children to come up with a riddle or two in which the subject is a door. What clues can be given to the reader without giving too much away? Discuss ideas in class first.

- **Descriptive sentences:** Invite the children to write several sentences which contain one or more of the descriptive words listed in the word banks above.

Long task | Fiction

- **Science-fiction story:** Ask the children to write a short story in which they, and some friends, stumble across these modern-looking security doors. Against their better judgement they enter – and find themselves in a strange and mysterious high-tech laboratory, about to be experimented upon…

- **Descriptive writing:** Invite the pupils to write a longer piece of descriptive prose in which they open a door that leads to somewhere that they fear. What is the atmosphere like? How do they feel? What can they see? Is it as bad as they expected?

Short task | Non-Fiction

- **Writing clues:** Think back to the 20 questions game. This time invite the children to choose one person or thing that may lie behind the door and then write down 20 clues about that person or object. Will the others solve the mystery of who, or what, is lurking behind the door?

- **Explanations:** Ask the children to write about a particular door – either real or fictional – which they would fear to open. It could lead to e.g. an examination room, a dentist's surgery, a lion's cage, etc. Encourage them to give explanations for their fears.

Long task | Non-Fiction

- **Personal writing:** Ask the children to imagine that the doors in the picture are stage doors, which are usually located at the back of a theatre, so that stars can leave undisturbed. If the children were waiting outside, who would they most like to see come through these doors, and why?

- **Fire safety instructions:** Look together at the fire safety instructions which are usually located on or next to classroom doors. Invite the children to write similar instructions to put on their front or back doors at home.

Extension

- **Discursive/explanatory texts:** Discuss together what we mean when we say doors are closing for us, or opening up. Introduce/revisit the idea of career choices. If any 'door' was open to them, to become anything they wanted to be, what would they choose, and why? Share written explanations.

Name _____ Date _____

DREAM DOORS

Imagine that the doors in the picture open into a dream –
the best dream you could imagine.

What would it be? Where would it be set? What would
happen? Write some sentences to describe what you
might find on the other side.

_____

_____

_____

_____

_____

_____

_____

_____

_____

_____

_____

_____

Introduction

- Brainstorm the first words that enter the children's heads when they look at this image. Record these on the board and invite explanations for them.

- How do the children think this image was created? Share theories and ideas. What does it remind them of?

Discussion

- Elicit the children's knowledge and experience of computer images. Where have they seen some interesting pictures and posters designed using computer technology? How effective is it?

- Discuss together what the children think this picture might have been used to advertise or communicate. Or is a piece of artwork in its own right?

Interaction

- Are our hands the most important parts of our bodies? Discuss this question in class, either as a free discussion or as a debate, with speakers proposing other important parts, e.g. brain, heart.

- Invite volunteers to sit in the 'hot seat' at the front of the class and answer questions in the role of the artist or designer of this picture. What did he/she have in mind at the time?

Hands © Giles Angel/Alamy

WORD BANK

- Introduce/revisit phrases that are based on parts of the body, e.g. *give me a hand, let's put our heads together, give a leg up, in two minds, he's got heart*. Invite the pupils to write down other examples and then share them in a plenary. Discuss the term *idiom*, and point out the phrases that are *metaphors*.

- If the children could sum up this image in one word, what would it be? You may wish to restrict their choices to abstract nouns only, e.g. *friendship, unity, welcome, life, needs, voice, help*.

WRITING ACTIVITIES

Fiction (Short task)

- **Making metaphors:** Invite the children to write down a sentence for each of the metaphors listed in their word banks above. Share these in class and check the metaphorical meaning of each one.

- **Hands poem:** Ask the children to plan and draft a short poem all about our hands, including the variety of things we use them for.

Fiction (Long task)

- **Short story:** Invite the children to plan and draft a short story in which someone cries for a 'helping hand', just when they need it most. It may be in a crisis or just before they make a bad decision. Perhaps this person is usually reluctant to ask for someone to give them a hand.

- **Descriptive writing:** Talk together about what the most impressive hands in the world might look like. Would they be slender and delicate, pretty and dainty, or large, muscular and well-worn? Invite the children to write a paragraph describing in detail the most impressive hands they can imagine. Focus on the smallest details.

Non-Fiction (Short task)

- **Captions:** Encourage the children to come up with a shortlist of possible captions to accompany this image, thinking back to earlier discussions about what it might communicate to readers. Share these in class and consider the most apt lines.

- **Annotated design:** If, in many thousands of years' time, we will have evolved physically, what might our hands look like? Ask the children to draw some new 'designs' and then annotate them with labels and information about their features, and the kinds of tasks they have evolved to do.

Non-Fiction (Long task)

- **Explanation:** Of all the uses for this image (e.g. CD cover, book cover, billboard poster, etc.), which for the children is the most convincing, and why? Encourage them to write about how they think this image should be used, with an explanation.

- **Persuasive flier:** Explain that (for this task) this image appears on the front cover of a flier that advertises a new dance show, full of disco-dancing and music. The children must write some persuasive text to accompany the picture, e.g. rave reviews, highlights of the show, etc.

Extension

- **Personal writing:** How will humans use their hands in generations to come? Will we still need to do anything manually? Or will we have special buttons to press for every conceivable job? Encourage the children to write about how much they think our lives will have changed in the year 2507.

COMING TO A CINEMA NEAR YOU...

You have been asked to design a poster for a scary new film to be shown in cinemas around the UK, called *The Hand*.

Draw a picture to promote this movie and then write some powerful text to persuade readers to go and see the film.

Think especially about:

- colour
- font size and shape
- images of characters/settings
- exciting special effects
- scary scenes and events.

Introduction

- Ask the children to share their initial responses to this image. What are the first words that pop into their heads?

- Establish that these are hippos – short for *hippopotamuses*. Write the word on the board and discuss the alternative plural, *hippopotami*.

Discussion

- Elicit the children's knowledge and experience of hippopotamuses. Where have they seen them? Can they remember what they were like?

- Consider together where this photograph might have been taken. Encourage the children to 'see' the rest of the landscape. Share thoughts in class.

Interaction

- Working in pairs, invite the children to play 'word tennis' in which they sit opposite one another and take turns to call out a different animal name, until someone makes a fault through hesitation or repetition.

- Invite volunteers to sit in the 'hot seat' at the front of the class and answer questions in the role of one of the hippopotamuses in the picture! How do they feel? What kind of a day do they have planned?

Hippos © Lynne M Stone/Alamy

WORD BANK

- Look again at the image and invite the children to make a list of words that sum up the mood of this image, e.g. *friendship, togetherness, contentment, happiness, laziness,* etc. Share ideas in class, checking spelling each time.

- Invite the children to write down adjectives that capture not only the appearance, but also the character of the hippopotamus. Share these in class.

WRITING ACTIVITIES

Short task — Fiction

- **Acrostic:** Invite the children to draft an acrostic poem using the word *hippopotamus* as the vertical keyword. Encourage them to try to capture the character of the hippo – you may wish to discuss personification in class first.

- **Descriptive writing:** Think together about what the rest of the scene may look like (refer to previous discussions if appropriate). Then invite the children to write a short descriptive paragraph in which they describe the swamp which the hippos call home.

Short task — Non-Fiction

- **Captions:** Consider together what sort of lines could accompany this photograph, were it to appear in a magazine or as a poster, e.g. '*There's nothing like a good friend,*' or '*It's your turn to make the tea, dear.*'

- **Similarities and differences:** Ask the children to write down some similarities and differences between hippos and rhinos. Share these in class. You may wish to lead into research work, using websites and books, ready for the longer non-fiction tasks below.

Long task — Fiction

- **Animal adventure:** Invite the children to plan and draft a short story in which one or more hippos escape from a safari park, and find themselves in a nearby town centre, where, at last, they can do some shopping...

- **Character studies:** Ask the children to write character profiles for these hippos, and other animals in the zoo. Focus on appearance, personality, behaviour, likes and dislikes, role in the zoo, appeal to visitors, etc. You may wish for them to name their animals too!

Long task — Non-Fiction

- **Factfile card:** Invite the pupils to design a factfile card that might appear on the perimeter fence around the hippo enclosure, providing interesting facts about the hippo (e.g. origin, size and weight, diet, habitat, etc.). Use websites and animal encyclopaedias to source the information.

- **Presentation:** Ask the children to write and rehearse a two-minute presentation on a given zoo animal, focusing on origin, size, weight, diet, etc. Share presentations in class and appraise performances.

❶ Extension

- **Personification:** Introduce/revisit personification. Then ask the children to write sentences which describe different zoo animals in ways that personify them, giving them human attributes covering their movement, personality, behaviour and habits.

Name _____ Date _____

A HIPPO'S DREAM

Look again at the picture of the hippopotamuses, sleeping soundly in their cosy mud bath. What do you think they might be dreaming about?

Think for a few moments and then describe a dream they might be having, in a few sentences below.

_____

_____

_____

_____

_____

_____

_____

_____

_____

_____

_____

_____

Year 6/ HOUSES OF PARLIAMENT

Introduction

- Ask the children to share their initial responses to this image. Which city was it taken in? How do we know?
- Consider together what event is being celebrated in the picture, e.g. bonfire night, New Year celebrations, Queen's birthday, etc.

Discussion

- Elicit the children's knowledge and experience of this building, and government generally. Discuss the chambers at Westminster: the House of Commons and the House of Lords. Discuss the differences.
- Discuss the relevance of bonfire night to this particular building. Share knowledge of the Gunpowder Plot. What might have happened had Guy Fawkes succeeded?

Interaction

- Working in pairs, the children role-play a short scene in which one person is Guy Fawkes, plotting to blow up the Houses of Parliament, while the other is an acquaintance, who tries to discourage him from seeing it through!
- In pairs again, this time the children role-play a short scene in which one is the Prime Minister and another is an interviewer. Questions can be on anything they think is appropriate, and may include likes and dislikes, hopes and aspirations for the country, personal goals, etc.

Houses of Parliament
© image100/Alamy

WORD BANK

- Ask the children to write down descriptive words that capture the splendour of this building, both its exterior, and how the children imagine it to look inside. Share vocabulary in class and check spelling.
- Discuss the language of formal speeches, with terms including: *motion, This House believes, Chairman, Ladies and Gentlemen, Proposers and Opposers,* etc.

WRITING ACTIVITIES

Fiction

- **Sounds poem:** Invite the children to write a poem in which they explore onomatopoeic words associated with a firework display.
- **Descriptive writing:** Ask the pupils to write a short descriptive piece in which they describe a bonfire party, perhaps the one in the picture in London, from a spectator's viewpoint. Encourage them to think about the sounds, smells and sights of the evening – and the weather!

Non-Fiction

- **Newspaper headlines:** Ask the children to write a shortlist of interesting newspaper headlines that might accompany this particular picture, covering a special event in the calendar, e.g. New Year's Eve in London, or a one-off celebration.
- **Short information text:** Invite the children to write a short entry in an imaginary children's encyclopaedia, under the words 'Houses of Parliament'. What does this phrase mean? Where is this building and what is it used for?

Fiction

- **Adventure story:** Invite the children to plan and draft a short story in which an amazing party is planned for the PM, which involves firework displays over Parliament and other exciting events, e.g. a helter-skelter down Big Ben, paint-balling through Westminster corridors, etc!
- **Historical story/comic strip:** Ask the children to write up the story of Guy Fawkes and the Gunpowder Plot as a short story or comic book. Discuss the main events in class before the children set to work.

Non-Fiction

- **Postcard from London:** Invite the children to draft a postcard from London, with a similar image to this one on the front and a short message to family or friends on the reverse, with the appropriate address.
- **Debate speech:** Explain to the children that you are going to hold a class debate on the following motion: *This House believes that fireworks should be banned from private use. Displays should be run by professionals for the safety and enjoyment of others.* Discuss this motion and then ask the children to write a speech either for or against it.

Extension

- **Personal writing:** Invite the children to write about what they would do if they were in Government, as the newly appointed Education Secretary. What changes would they make to school life, and why? Share these thoughts in class and discuss.

ALIEN STORY

Look again at the picture of the fireworks over Westminster. Imagine that these are actually lights or explosions from an alien spacecraft, that has come to Earth.

Put these ideas into a plan for a science-fiction story, in which aliens come to London. What will happen? Are they friend or foe?

Think about characters, setting and plot.

Characters:

Story Setting(s):

Plot:

Beginning

Middle

End

Now see if you can write up your alien story!

Year 6/JET FIGHTER

Introduction

- Ask the children to share their initial responses to this image. Record any interesting words or phrases on the board.

- Looking closely at the image, where do the children think this jet may be flying? Share ideas, as the children 'see' the landscape below.

Discussion

- Consider together how it must feel to soar across the sky in a jet fighter like this one. Share words and phrases in class.

- Can anyone identify what kind of plane this is? Elicit the children's prior knowledge of aeroplanes, and particularly military ones. Is this European, American, or from some other country in the world? How can we tell?

Interaction

- Invite volunteers to come and sit in the 'hot seat' and answer questions in the role of the pilot of this aeroplane. Where is he/she flying to? What is the mission he/she has been given?

- In pairs or discussion groups, encourage the children to share their own experiences of flying, or their hopes and preconceptions if they have not yet flown.

Jet Fighter © Puresteock/Alamy

WORD BANK

- Ask the children to make a list of interesting verbs and adverbs to describe the movement of this aeroplane in the sky, e.g. *soaring, diving, dipping, gliding.*

- Brainstorm the technical terms and phrases used to describe the features of an aeroplane like this one. Check spelling together. (E.g. *cockpit, jet engines, undercarriage.*)

WRITING ACTIVITIES

Short task Fiction

- **Descriptive poem:** Invite the children to draft a short descriptive poem which describes the feeling of soaring across the sky in a jet plane. Consider together the sights, sounds and the feeling of travelling so fast high above the Earth. Encourage them to use similes and metaphors wherever possible (e.g. *like a bullet*).

- **Descriptive writing:** Ask the pupils to write a short descriptive piece in which they describe an imaginary first flight in a jet plane like this one. Focus particularly on the exhilaration on take-off.

Long task Fiction

- **Adventure story:** Invite the children to plan and draft a short story in which they have recently been recruited to join an elite flying squadron. Within a few weeks of joining up, the country declares war on another, and they are out flying real missions over enemy territory.

- **Science-fiction story:** Ask the children to plan and draft a short story set in the future, where all of us are commuting to work or visiting shops and schools in aeroplanes and hover jets. Share ideas and possible plot lines for the story in class.

Short task Non-Fiction

- **Captions:** Invite the class to come up with interesting lines to write underneath this photograph. Imagine it appeared in a magazine or newspaper. Discuss possible scenarios, e.g. to recruit new pilots into the Army/RAF; to announce a new jet fighter on the scene, etc.

- **Personal writing:** What would be the children's first choice of transport, if they could ride in any vehicle or vessel at all – and why? Share writing in class.

Long task Non-Fiction

- **Annotated design:** Invite the pupils to come up with their own annotated designs for a super new jet plane, fit for the year 2050. Encourage them to label its new features and functions. Ask for volunteers to present their work and talk about their designs to the class.

- **Discussion text:** Should we be spending so much money on hi-tech defence systems and armoury when there are still people living in poverty in this country and throughout the world? Which is more important? Encourage the children to explore both sides of this debate.

Extension

- **Information text:** Invite the class to conduct research into the types of aeroplanes we currently have in our armed forces, using the Internet, encyclopaedias and magazines. Ask them to present this information in the form of either a two-minute presentation or a written information text, with illustrations, diagrams, labels and text.

Name _____ Date _____

FLY ME TO THE MOON...

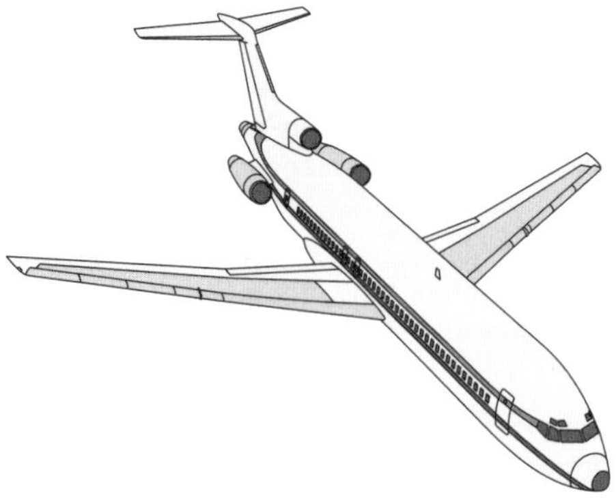

If you could be flown to anywhere in the world (or beyond) where would you go, and why?

Write down the name of the destination in the box below and then give some reasons to explain your choice.

Finish off with an illustration of your chosen place.

The place I would fly to is _____

I would like to travel there because _____

_____

_____

_____

_____

_____

Introduction

- Ask the children to share their initial responses to this image. Record any interesting words or phrases on the board.

- Look closely at the image: can anyone ascertain where it was taken? Inside somewhere looking out, or the reverse?

Discussion

- Consider together what exactly might be on the other side of this door. Can anyone make out the features?

- What effect does this image have on the children? How do they feel when they see it? Encourage individuals to articulate how they feel when they look at the image (e.g. *curious, trapped, lonely*).

Interaction

- In pairs, the children play '20 questions' by asking one another to think of a place (or person) that is through the keyhole. The other must guess who or what by asking 20 questions, the answers to which can only be *yes* or *no*.

- Invite the children to consider what is on this side of the door – i.e. behind the camera. Share thoughts in class, encouraging the children to 'see' the setting.

Through the Keyhole
© Samdea Photo/Alamy

WORD BANK

- Ask the children to write down words and phrases to describe the landscape that lies through the keyhole. Focus not only on what they can see (and imagine), but also the mood of the place: the effect it has on our emotions.

- What season is this? How can we tell? Invite the children to make four short lists of descriptive words to describe this scene (and what they can see in their mind's eye) in each of the four seasons.

WRITING ACTIVITIES

Fiction
(Short task)

- **Riddles:** Invite the class to draft riddles to show what might be lurking through a keyhole. The lines of the verses will give small clues about the setting, without giving the place away too soon! Draft a riddle in class together first.

- **Descriptive writing:** Ask the pupils to write a paragraph of descriptive prose, based on the setting that lies beyond the door. Think about the sights, sounds, smells and the atmosphere.

Fiction
(Long task)

- **Mystery story:** Invite the children to plan and draft a short story in which they, and some friends, stumble across an old estate, with an old mansion house surrounded by sinister looking forests and scrubland. Against their better judgement they scale the locked gates and enter…

- **Story beginning:** Ask the pupils to choose a new location in their mind for what lies through the keyhole. Then invite them to write the beginning of a story, set in this location. The opening paragraphs introduce the reader to the place.

Non-Fiction
(Short task)

- **Captions:** Invite the class to come up with interesting lines to write underneath this photograph. Imagine that it appears as an advert for a new film or novel entitled *What Lies Beyond*.

- **Keyhole clues:** Invite the children to bring in photos of themselves. Mix these up and give them out, each one clipped to a sheet of paper with a small keyhole cut out in the centre. They must guess who it is by moving the keyhole around the picture! Ask them to note down the features as they see them: e.g. *green eyes, blonde hair,* etc.

Non-Fiction
(Long task)

- **Personal writing:** Encourage the children to write up their chosen theories about what lies behind the camera taking this image, on this side of the door. They must settle for one theory, one place, and then give a factual account of it.

- **Radio advertisement:** Refer back to the film poster mentioned in the captions task above. Ask the children to draft the opening to a radio advert for this new film. Remember they have no visuals, so the script must develop listeners' curiosity in the same way that the poster of the keyhole does.

Extension

- **Descriptive prose:** Invite the children to imagine that they are imprisoned inside an old castle keep, gazing out through the keyhole of the great oak door that stands between them and the world outside. How do they feel? Will they ever get out? How do they see (and think of) the world now, through this tiny spy hole?

Name _____ Date _____

COMPOUND WORDS

If look at the word *keyhole* you will see that it is actually made up of two separate words. It is, after all, the hole which you put your key in!

This is an example of a *compound word*. Can you think of any more?

Make a list of compound words and write their meanings.

Compound word	Meaning

Introduction

- Ask the children to share their initial responses to this image. What can they see? Share observations in class.

- Count the number of boats the children can see in the picture. What are the lights coming from? Is there a boardwalk connecting the boats? Can anyone see the mainland/dockside?

Discussion

- Explore together theories about where this photograph may have been taken. Has anyone seen a harbour like this one? Elicit the children's knowledge and experience of places such as this.

- Consider together why there is so much fog. At what time of day might this shot have been taken? How can we tell?

Interaction

- In pairs or small discussion groups, invite the children to imagine they are present at the harbour as the photograph is being taken. What can they see, hear and smell? Encourage them to articulate their thoughts aloud.

- In pairs, the children think of other locations they have seen/visited which would look equally mysterious and exciting in the mist. Share these in class, e.g. *Dartmoor, Sherwood Forest, Warwick Castle, Tintagel*. Then children use interesting vocabulary to describe these places.

Misty Harbour
© Troy & Mary
Parlee/Alamy

WORD BANK

- Revisit/introduce adjectival phrases by showing examples on the board. Ask the children to come up with interesting phrases of their own to sum up the mood and atmosphere of this time and place, e.g. *shrouded in mist; eerie and quiet; cold and unwelcoming*.

- Revisit similes and metaphors. Invite the children to create their own to describe the dramatic effects of the mist and fog on the landscape, e.g. *like a pea soup; boats wrapped in cotton wool*.

WRITING ACTIVITIES

Short task | Fiction

- **Figurative poem:** Invite the children to refer to the metaphors and similes listed in their word banks. Ask them to write a short poem which describes this misty harbour in figurative ways. Brainstorm the opening lines in class and then share pupils' work at the end.

- **Story beginnings:** Invite the children to draft the opening paragraph(s) of an imaginary story set in this location. Discuss different ways of beginning a story, e.g. dialogue, narrated action, description, etc.

Long task | Fiction

- **Ghost story:** Invite the children to plan and draft a short story in which they, or some other central character(s) charter an old fishing boat, which they soon discover is haunted by an old fisherman who died on board many years ago...

- **Adventure story:** Ask the children to refer to a different location, discussed earlier, which becomes enveloped in thick fog. Ask them to base an adventure story on this setting, in which they become stranded in dense fog, with no obvious signs of rescue.

Non-Fiction

Short task |

- **Glossary:** Invite the children to draft a short excerpt from a nautical glossary, in which some basic boating terms are listed and defined. These may be known already to the pupils, or they may find them in dictionaries and encyclopaedias, e.g. *bow, stern, boardwalk, galley, hull, knots*.

- **Weather terms:** How many weather terms can the children think of? Encourage them (in pairs or individually) to write down words associated with the weather. Then share and check spellings. These will be useful for the Wordsearch activity on the opposite page.

Non-Fiction

Long task |

- **Weather chart:** Invite the children to construct a weather chart, which shows the different types of weather experienced in this country, with an arrow or other kind of system that shows the weather today. Encourage them to find innovative ways of displaying the day's weather.

- **Journalistic text:** Invite the children to draft a page from a local newspaper, reporting the 'pea souper' that descended on the coastal town when this photo was taken. Encourage them to include local eye-witness accounts, weather reports and historical references to similar weather in the past.

Extension

- **Weather reports:** Invite the children to research the language of weather reports. How are they structured? Are there standard phrases that are used each time, for each type of weather? Research written weather reports in newspapers and online. Then invite the pupils to draft their own '24-hour forecast'.

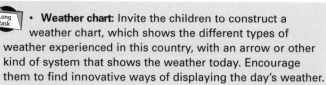

Name _____ Date _____

WEATHER WORDSEARCH

Look again at the weather words you wrote down in an earlier writing task.

Can you fit these into a Wordsearch? See how many of these words you can hide in the grid below. Then see if your friends can find them. Keep a note of the hidden words on the lines below.

Weather Words

_____ _____ _____

_____ _____ _____

_____ _____ _____

_____

Introduction

- Ask the children to share their initial responses to this image. How can they tell that this is unlikely to be somewhere in Great Britain? (E.g. *style of housing; dry, rocky landscape*.)

- Challenge the children to count the different colours they can see in this image. Share answers in class.

Discussion

- Establish that this photograph was taken in Nepal. Elicit the children's prior knowledge of Nepal. Where is it in the world? What is it famous for? (E.g. *Everest, Buddhist monasteries, sherpas*.)

- Would the children like to live in such a location? What might it be like? Share thoughts and responses in class, encouraging them to 'experience' the landscape.

Interaction

- Which other extreme locations like this one have the children visited or seen in books/films, where townships have grown? (E.g. *desert towns, Italian citadels high on rocky hills*.) Share observations and experiences in group discussions, and then a feedback plenary.

- Word tennis: Invite pairs of volunteers to sit at the front and play word tennis, using countries of the world. Players sit opposite one another and take turns to call out a different country of the world until someone falters through hesitation or repetition. Change to cities/mountain ranges/coastal towns.

Nepalese Town
© Andrew Wrighting/
Alamy

WORD BANK

- Encourage the children to consider how different this location might be in deepest winter, when the town is cut off from the outside world and enveloped in snow drifts and freezing cold temperatures. Then ask them to compile two lists of descriptive phrases, to describe this place in summer/winter.

- Revisit prepositions, by highlighting how this town is high above sea-level, but below Everest. Ask the pupils to see how many prepositions they can write down in two minutes. Then share.

WRITING ACTIVITIES

Fiction

- **Descriptive sentences:** Ask the children to write sentences that contain the descriptive words and phrases listed in their word banks, describing this location in different weather conditions and seasons.

- **Haiku:** Introduce/revisit haiku poems (three-lined poems with a 5-7-5 syllabic pattern). Then encourage the children to draft their own haiku on the subject of Everest, or a Nepalese town.

Non-Fiction

- **Diary extract:** Invite the children to imagine that they are taking part in a trek to Nepal, and stopping at this town for the night. They write a short diary entry, describing the town and surrounding landscape in a few lines.

- **Personal writing:** Encourage the children to write a short written response to the following question: If the children could live anywhere in the world, where would they choose, and why?

Fiction

- **Fantasy adventure:** Invite the children to plan and draft a short story set in the mountains of Nepal, where, according to legend, the last remaining dragon lives, with her offspring. The central character of the story sets out on a quest to catch the dragon for the world's first Dragon Safari Park.

- **Fictional recount:** Encourage the pupils to draft a fictional recount of an expedition to Everest. Discuss the possible challenges and events in class first, then share recounts in a final plenary.

Non-Fiction

- **Postcard from Nepal:** Ask the children to design and write an imaginary postcard from Nepal, sent home during an expedition there with friends.

- **Discussion text:** Should so many people be allowed to trek through the Himalayas every year? Is it too dangerous? Are we intruding on nature, and on the lives of the local Nepalese? Or are visitors bringing much-needed custom to the area? Ask the children to explore the issues.

Extension

- **Persuasive writing:** Ask the children to plan and draft a persuasive holiday brochure in which this location is advertised as the ideal destination for the intrepid tourist. Focus on spectacular walks and climbs, rich and welcoming culture and customs, and unique accommodation. Encourage the pupils to make good use of visual and written forms of information.

LETTER TO A PEN FRIEND

Imagine that the town in the picture is twinned with your own town or city.

Your school has launched a plan to pair up each pupil with a pen pal from a school in the Nepalese township.

Write a letter to your new pen friend, telling them all about yourself. Remember to mention the things that they might find particularly interesting or unusual (like traffic jams and giant supermarkets!).

Dear _____

_____

_____

_____

_____

_____

_____

_____

_____

_____

_____

Continue on a separate sheet if necessary.

Introduction

- Ask the children to share their initial responses to this image. When do they think it was taken?

- Look for clues in the image to date it, e.g. sepia colour, old fashioned clothes, furniture, etc.

Discussion

- Discuss together how fashions have changed over the years. What would someone wear today if they wanted to look smart? How is it different from this style of dress? (E.g. different suit, tie, shirt, perhaps no hat, etc.)

- Track the thoughts of this man by inviting volunteers to call out lines of speech, assuming the man's viewpoint. What can he see? Does he want to be there? Is he getting impatient, perhaps?

Interaction

- In pairs, the children discuss theories about who this man may have been. What did he do for a living? Why was this photograph taken, and when?

- Invite volunteers to come to the 'hot seat' and answer questions from the class in the role of the man in the photograph. What stories could he tell? What might his life be like, compared to ours?

Old Photograph
© bildagentur-online.com/historypix/
Alamy

WORD BANK

- Consider together why we often say 'cheese' for the camera – i.e. it creates the right shape for a smile! Invite the children to think of other words that would do the same thing. Say them aloud.

- Encourage the children to consider which words and phrases might be alien to this man – words which have evolved with modern living. Make a list individually, and then as a class. E.g. *texting, DVD, online, e-mailing, fax.*

WRITING ACTIVITIES

Fiction

- **Acrostic poem:** Invite the children to write an acrostic using the word *photograph*. Focus particularly on the 'cheesy' words referred to in the word banks, as the subject is asked to 'smile for the camera'. How do we feel when we are forced to hold a smile?

- **Character study:** Consider together how a photograph can say a thousand words. What stories can this photograph tell us? Ask the children to write down a few sentences about this man, based on what they observe from the photograph.

Fiction

- **Historical story:** Invite the children to plan and draft a story set in Victorian times. Focus on what they know about this era, and try to include historical references that are accurate for the time. Discuss possible plot lines and settings, e.g. children break out of a workhouse, or pupils take over the class of a very strict schoolmaster!

- **Science-fiction story:** Ask the children to plan and draft a short story in which the central character travels back in time to a previous era, e.g. Victorian times. What happens when they get there? Could they bring this man back with them? What would he think of modern life?

Non-Fiction

- **Annotated sketch:** If the children had to dress very smartly for a photograph today, what would they wear, and why? Encourage them to sketch their 'photograph outfit' and then annotate it with labels.

- **Personal writing:** How do the children feel when they have their photograph taken on their own – perhaps posing for a school photo? Do they enjoy it? Do they dread it? Do they usually blink just at the wrong moment? Encourage them to write a paragraph of their thoughts.

Non-Fiction

- **Modern dictionary:** Ask the children to refer to the modern words listed in their word banks – words and phrases which may be alien to this man. Then invite them to write definitions that someone from a previous era would understand. Share these in class.

- **Explanation text:** Ask the children to choose one item of modern living, like a television or mobile for example, and then write a brief explanation of how it works, so that this man would understand the process. Encourage the pupils to choose something of which they have a basic knowledge.

Extension

- **Captions:** Encourage the children to make a shortlist of captions that could accompany this image, were it to appear as an advertisement for some item or service, in a magazine, either years ago or today. Share captions in class and discuss the effects that this image would have on readers.

Name _____ Date _____

A VERY DIFFERENT KIND OF CAMERA!

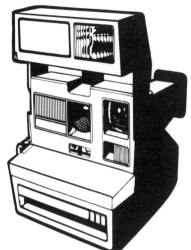

Imagine a very different kind of camera: one which takes a snapshot of your face and then converts it into a detailed, written description of your features. What would it say about you?

Have a go! Write a 'written image' of yourself, so that someone who has never met you would get an accurate impression of your face.

You may need to use a mirror to remind yourself of the finer details of your face, from close up!

A written image of me

_____

_____

_____

_____

_____

_____

_____

_____

_____

_____

Now swap these around and see if others can guess who it is!

Mind's Eye/Writing   Year 6/OLD PHOTOGRAPH

Introduction

- Ask the children to share their initial responses to this image. Are the riders coming into view or leaving the scene?

- Consider together where this may have been taken. Look closely at the image again. What can be seen on the horizon? Is this a black and white image or colour? How can we tell?

Discussion

- Discuss together where these riders may be going/have come from. Are they riding for pleasure or are they patrolling or guarding something or somewhere?

- Elicit the children's knowledge and experience of horse-riding. Invite volunteers to share their experiences, describing the excitement of riding horses.

Interaction

- Encourage the children to imagine the rest of this setting, then invite volunteers to describe the scene for the class – looking behind the camera and to the left and right.

- Invite volunteers to come to the 'hot seat' and answer questions in the role of one of the riders in the picture. Where are they going? How refreshing does it feel to be riding horses so close to the ocean?

Riders
© image100/Alamy

WORD BANK

- Invite the children to compile a list of interesting adjectives to describe this scene. Encourage them to divide the lists into five categories, one for each of the senses. Share in class.

- Revisit/introduce onomatopoeia. Brainstorm words together that capture the sounds of the sea, and especially the sounds these riders may make near the water's edge, e.g. *splashing, clip-clopping* etc.

WRITING ACTIVITIES

Short task — Fiction

- **Onomatopoeic poem:** Invite the children to draft a short poem about the seaside. Encourage them to make good use of the onomatopoeic words in their word banks. Focus on words with soft consonants, e.g.: *satin sand, splashing around, salty seas and sharp shingle*.

- **Descriptive prose:** Invite the children to draft a short paragraph describing this scene from the viewpoint of one of the riders. Encourage them to focus on the sights, sounds and smells of the seaside, and the feel of galloping across the windswept beach.

Long task — Fiction

- **Song lyrics:** Invite the children to draft two verses and a chorus for an imaginary song about riding horses near the sea. Encourage them to use the descriptive words in their word banks. Focus on how to create a rhyming, repeating chorus, by modelling this in class.

- **Seaside adventure:** Ask the pupils to draft a short story about a trip to the seaside. Suggest that the central characters enjoy a donkey ride on the beach, but stray too far from where they should be. Where will their donkey take them? Will they become stranded by the tide?

Short task — Non-Fiction

- **Personal writing:** If the children could ride a pony anywhere in the world, where would they go pony trekking, and why? Share dream destinations, each speaker explaining their choice to the class. Think especially about places that would be difficult to trek through on foot, without help.

- **Written account:** Invite the children to think again about why these riders are in the picture, where they are going, and so on. Then encourage them to write up their thoughts and share them in class.

Long task — Non-Fiction

- **Safety instructions:** Invite the children to design and produce a poster informing children how to stay safe when playing by the seaside. Discuss safety precautions in class first, e.g. *stay in sight of an adult; don't paddle beyond your depth, keep track of the tide times*, etc.

- **Discussion text:** Ask the pupils to write a short text in which they discuss the different pursuits people engage in at the seaside. Why do people like to be by the sea so much? Finish with an editorial on what they, as the writer, most like to do at the seaside.

Extension

- **Playscript:** Invite the children to plan and draft an excerpt from an imaginary playscript. The scene for them to write involves them on a beach, when they are confronted by two strangers on horseback. Where have they come from? Where are they going? Are they real or could they be ghost riders?

JOIN THE ADVENTURE!

You are the managing director of a new holiday company, called 'All-Action Adventures', that organises activity trips for children.

Write the **opening paragraph** for a brand new brochure advertising trips to a new activity centre on the south coast, where the children will be able to go horse-riding, coarse fishing, sailing, and lots more!

Remember to keep your introduction lively, punchy and packed full of persuasive adjectives and imperatives.

_____

_____

_____

_____

_____

_____

_____

_____

_____

_____

Continue on a separate sheet if necessary.

Introduction

- Ask the children to share their initial responses to this image. Record any initial words and phrases that enter the children's heads. These can be explored in a later plenary.

- Look closely at the image. How much of the human head has become robotic? What might you call a figure like this? Is it male of female? Or neither? Think of some interesting names (e.g. *android, humanbot, robowoman*).

Discussion

- Consider how, and why, this image was created. Is it from a film, perhaps. Share knowledge and experiences of similar figures in science-fiction films and books.

- Discuss, as a class, or in groups, ways in which this robowoman might be superior to us (e.g. *speed of thought processing, strength and efficiency*), and ways in which she may not, (e.g. *emotions, intuition, relationships,* etc.).

Interaction

- Working in pairs, the children think of theories and explanations for this picture, e.g. what film/book/magazine it is from, what the name of this character is, etc. Share these in class.

- Invite volunteers to come to the 'hot seat' and answer questions in the role of this robowoman. How old is she? What year in the future is she from? What is her purpose? Are there others like her?

Robowoman
© Colin Anderson/Alamy

WORD BANK

- Ask the pupils to write down some of the words discussed earlier, which are suitable names for this figure. Invite them to make up their own terms and explain them to the class. Ask them to construct fictional compound words from established words, prefixes and suffixes, e.g. *robowoman*.

- Invite the children to write down adjectives to describe the capabilities of this figure. Then look at comparative and superlative endings, e.g. *the fastest, most efficient, strongest robot in the world*.

WRITING ACTIVITIES

Fiction

- **Brainstorm:** Consider together the kind of words and phrases that are associated with the logical processing of computer-based technology and robots, e.g. *illogical, affirmative, negative, malfunctioning,* and so on. Write these down.

- **Robot poem:** Invite the children to use the brainstorm words to construct a poem in which a robot thinks/speaks using functional, robotic language rather than creative or figurative words. Evocative, thought-provoking and emotive language is not wanted in this poem!

Fiction

- **Science-fiction story:** Ask the children to plan and draft a short story set in the future, in a world in which humans live alongside (or in subservience to) robots, like the one in the image. Will the main character find a way to reclaim human supremacy over the androids?

- **Robot narrative:** Ask the children to choose a favourite story and rewrite the opening paragraph(s) in robot style language, omitting rich adjectives, similes and metaphors and presenting the information in a more functional, factual way. Consider together what is lost.

Non-Fiction

- **Captions:** Invite the pupils to think of interesting captions to accompany this image. It can be based on a newspaper account, a magazine article, a book cover or some form of advertisement. Share ideas in class. How does the language link to the image?

- **Factual descriptions:** Ask the children to write a short factual description of the robot's name, its functions and features. This can be set out in 'robotic' language, e.g. with different categories and fields – *height: 2.15m; IQ: 1050; virtual brain capacity: 5000cc: speed: 150mph; function: to transmit knowledge to infant Earthlings.*

Non-Fiction

- **Journalistic text:** Ask the children to write an exciting newspaper story in which this robot is heralded as the world's first robohuman, half-human, half-android, created by a professor and his/her team in a secret laboratory. What will be the reaction of the rest of the world? Include quotations and reactions from interested parties and experts.

- **Discussion text:** Will this ever happen? Will robot technology become so advanced that ailing humans will be rebuilt as robohumans, with body parts replaced with super-powered bionic technology? The children explore the issues and ethics.

Extension

- **Information text:** Invite the children to produce a short information text, showing the different ways in which robotics currently influences our lives, and how much more of a role robots may have in the future. Encourage them to source information from encyclopaedias, Internet sites and sci-fi magazines.

MISSION IMPOSSIBLE

Look again at the picture. Imagine that Robowoman is looking straight at you because you are the Creator, the one who made her and the one who is about to announce her next assignment.

What will it be? Write down Robowoman's next mission.

Robowoman, your next mission is...

_____

_____

_____

_____

_____

_____

_____

_____

_____

_____

_____

_____

_____

_____

_____

Introduction

- Ask the children to share their initial responses to this image. Write down any words that the children articulate on the board and discuss them.

- Look closely at this image and identify facts about it: number of carriages, number of people in each row, number of legs, etc.

Discussion

- Consider together where this image may have been taken. Does anyone recognise this roller coaster? Is it in this country?

- Elicit the children's knowledge and experience of roller coasters, and theme parks generally. Which places have the children visited in the UK, and abroad? What were the places like? Share feedback.

Interaction

- Invite volunteers who have been on a similar roller coaster to express how they felt at the time. As the children describe the experience to their peers, encourage others to explain if they would like to try it or not. Consider why some of us enjoy taking risks and the thrill of being scared.

- Ask for volunteers to sit in the 'hot seat' and answer questions in the role of a passenger on the roller coaster. Can they describe the feeling of being hurled upside down and thrown around at speed?

Roller Coaster
© Phil Degginer/Alamy

WORD BANK

- Revisit alliteration in class. Ask the children to come up with some interesting, alliterative names for different rides in an imaginary theme park or fairground, e.g. *Devil's Drop, Cowboy Carousel*.

- Invite the children to write down adjectives to describe the speed of the roller coaster, e.g. *rapid, hurtling, breathtaking*.

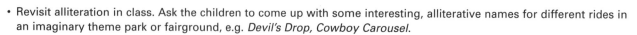

WRITING ACTIVITIES

Fiction
Short task

- **Visitors' comments:** Ask the children to refer to the adjectives in their word banks, and to write at least ten different lines of speech to describe how ten passengers might feel during the ride, e.g. *'Whoopee!' cried Michael, 'This is breathtaking!'* and *'Oh no!' sobbed Mum, 'It's stomach-churning!'*.

- **Shape poem:** Invite the children to plan and draft a short poem written in the shape of a roller coaster ride, with lines going up and down to simulate the tracks. Share these in class/display them on the interactive whiteboard.

Fiction
Long task

- **Science-fiction story:** Invite the pupils to plan and draft a short story in which the central character finds themselves on board the highest roller coaster in the world, during its debut circuit. Then a problem: one of the carriages is coming loose. It could become disconnected at any point…

- **Descriptive writing:** Ask the children to draft a paragraph or two of descriptive prose, in which they describe a roller coaster ride from the viewpoint of a passenger, for whom this is their first such ride. How do they feel? Focus on some particularly exciting, evocative words and phrases to capture the sights, sounds and feel of the ride.

Non-Fiction
Short task

- **Fairground rides:** Encourage the children to draw and label an invented ride at an imaginary fairground or theme park. Share in class.

- **Slogans:** Ask the children to imagine that this picture appears in an advert for a new theme park that has opened near their town. Invite them to shortlist some interesting slogans to write underneath it, advertising the theme park as a great day out. Focus on the thrills and scares in store.

Non-Fiction
Long task

- **Radio transcript:** Invite the children to draft a short transcript for a radio advertisement in which listeners are persuaded to visit a new theme park in the area – one with the largest roller coaster in Europe. Focus on the sights and sounds of the theme park.

- **Discussion text:** Why do people like going on roller coasters? Why are some people so thrilled by a sense of danger? What is it about human nature that makes us enjoy risks? Invite the children to explore both their own and other's views, in a discussion text about 'being a daredevil'.

Extension

- **Research and presentation:** Ask the children to conduct some research into the history of roller coasters specifically, and/or theme parks generally. Using books, encyclopaedias and Internet sites, the children put together a short information or non-chronological report, and oral presentation.

SAME RIDE, DIFFERENT RIDERS

Some people can ride the same roller coaster, but feel *very* differently about it!

See if you can sort out these adjectives into the two different categories below: one to describe the feelings of a confident roller coaster fan, and the other to show how a more nervous passenger might feel.

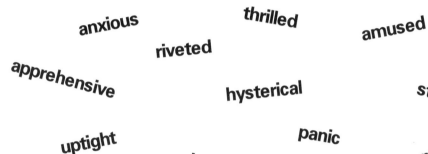

anxious thrilled amused

riveted

apprehensive hysterical stricken

relaxed

uptight panic gripped

daunted enthralled

entertained agitated

Roller coaster fan	Nervous passenger
_____	_____
_____	_____
_____	_____
_____	_____
_____	_____
_____	_____
_____	_____

Introduction

- Ask the children to share their initial responses to this image. Record any interesting key words on the board and discuss.
- Consider together what time of day this might have been taken. How can we tell?

Discussion

- Discuss where this image may have been taken. Could it be in this country? If so, what type of buildings might these be (e.g. temples, mosques)? Or is it somewhere else in the world?
- Consider what these buildings could be used for. Elicit the children's prior knowledge and experience of buildings of this type, especially religious ones. Encourage the children to share their experiences, and for others to listen and respond with positive questions and comments.

Interaction

- In discussion groups, invite the children to discuss why many religious buildings are often ornate in style and construction. Why are they so lavish? For whom are they built? Share views in a plenary.
- In pairs, the children interview one another to find out what, and where, is the most ornate building they have ever visited. Then invite the children to feed back to the class, speaking on behalf of their partners.

Roof Tops © Blimages/Alamy

WORD BANK

- Invite the children to write down the adjectives that come into their heads when they see this image. Then ask them to do the same for abstract nouns, e.g. *peace, religion, faith, beauty*. Share these in class and check for spelling.
- Revisit similes; ask the children to think up interesting similes and metaphors to describe the appearance and importance of these buildings, e.g. *like jewels on the horizon; towers of candy; like icing on a cake; sugar sculptures, like a crown in the sky.*

WRITING ACTIVITIES

Fiction

- **Rhymes and sayings:** Focus on the red sky in the image. Revisit/introduce the old saying, *'Red sky at night, shepherd's delight. Red sky in the morning, shepherd's warning.'* Discuss what this means. Then invite the children to create their own endings for the same phrases. Share in class.
- **Figurative poem:** Using the similes and metaphors in their word banks, invite the children to draft a short poem about these beautiful roof tops. Share these in class.

Non-Fiction

- **Factual description:** Can the children describe this image in words, to someone that cannot see it? Invite them to write a short factual account of what is in the picture, and particularly the shapes of the buildings.
- **Riddles:** Ask the children to think of an unusual building that is well known. Then invite them to write a list of clues which should help their peers in the class to guess which building they have thought of. Encourage them to make the clues intriguing and not too easy!

Fiction

- **Fantasy story:** Invite the pupils to plan and draft a short story set in a secluded, magical principality, where elaborate turrets and golden towers stretch into the sky, and the buildings are made of marble. Who lives there? No one else in the world has ever heard of this city, until now...
- **Science-fiction:** Ask the children to draft a science-fiction story, set on Mars, where the red sky looks down on a strange and advanced race of people. One day they receive a visit from the first human astronauts to set foot on the red planet. What happens?

Non-Fiction

- **Annotated design:** Ask the children to design the exterior for a new type of religious building, for any religion they wish to choose. Encourage them to annotate this with informative sentences to describe its features and the construction materials used to build it.
- **Personal writing:** *Should we all follow the same religion? Would it make life easier?* Or would the world be a much duller, unhappier place if we all had to follow one particular faith? Why do we have so many different religions? What do the children think? Invite them to write a thoughtful response to the opening question.

Extension

- **Character description:** Encourage the children to imagine that the bell towers and turrets in the picture belong to just one building – a giant, golden palace, home to a rich emperor. Ask them to write a character profile for this emperor, based on what they see in the picture and what they imagine beyond it.

BUILT IN THE YEAR 3007

Think about it. What materials will be used? How many people will live in the houses? How many shops will fit into the shopping centres? What will the new churches and temples look like?

Sketch a design for a 31st-century building. Then write about it in the space below.

_____

_____

_____

_____

_____

_____

Introduction

- Ask the children to share their initial responses to this image. What type of vehicle is this? Can anyone recognise it? Which way is it actually going?

- Look closely at the image. Where could it have been taken? What can be seen in this wing mirror? Is it the ocean in the distance, or mountain ranges? What is the weather like? Encourage the children to imagine the surrounding landscape.

Discussion

- Elicit the children's experience of being driven along dusty tracks or trekking through wild scenery. Share travel stories.

- Consider together where this vehicle may be going, or where it has come from. Why is it on the road? Could this be some holiday safari or coastal trek? Or is the driver working?

Interaction

- Invite volunteers to come to the front of the class and answer questions in the 'hot seat' as the driver of this vehicle.

- In pairs, the children discuss where in the world they would most like to go trekking, and why. Ask the pupils to feed back to the whole group, each person speaking on behalf of their partner.

Trekking © Brian Atkinson/Alamy

WORD BANK

- Invite the children to use all five senses to come up with a list of evocative words to describe the feeling of travelling through this beautiful landscape. Share these words.

- Revisit imperative verbs, in the context of advertising a car. E.g. *drive over mountains, see the world's great countryside; scale heights, cruise through valleys, take on rocky roads,* etc. Share words.

WRITING ACTIVITIES

 ## Fiction

- **Trekking poem:** Invite the children to draft a short poem *'Out of a window'* in which they describe a trekking adventure. Encourage them to choose a specific location (e.g. desert, coastal tracks, jungle) and then focus on the sights, sounds and smells along the way, as they peer out of their window.

- **Descriptive writing:** Ask the children to draft a short paragraph of descriptive prose in which they describe the scene in the photograph, using the ideas they had for their word bank.

 ## Non-Fiction

- **Slogans:** If this picture were to appear in a magazine for a 4x4 vehicle, what sort of slogan could accompany it? Share ideas and then encourage the children to come up with some more examples, e.g. *Stuck in traffic? Go off-road.*

- **Postcard:** Invite the children to design and produce a postcard which they might send to friends or family whilst on holiday, trekking across the desert or through the jungle, in a vehicle like this. How does it feel being thrown around in a 4x4?

 ## Fiction

- **Film storyboard:** Ask the children construct some opening film scenes on a storyboard, taking the scene in the photograph as the opening clip. What happens next? Who is in the vehicle? Are they being chased? Or are they rescuing someone? Share ideas, each child talking about the sequence of clips on their board.

- **Adventure story:** Invite the pupils to plan and draft a short story set in an extreme location, like a jungle, desert or mountain range. The writer, or another character, is on a trekking holiday, travelling around in a 4x4. One day, the vehicle breaks down, in a very remote area. What will happen next?

 ## Non-Fiction

- **Car brochure:** Ask the children to utilise the imperative verbs in their word banks to construct a short excerpt from an imaginary sales brochure, advertising a super new 4x4 vehicle, that can 'go anywhere'.

- **Discussion text:** Are there some places we shouldn't be allowed to visit by 4x4 vehicles, or should all beautiful places be available to visit in this way? Could we be causing damage to the environment we enjoy, with pollution and erosion from these vehicles? Encourage the children to explore both sides of this issue.

 ## Extension

- **Research and presentation:** Encourage the children to conduct research into a particular make of 4x4 vehicle (e.g. Landrover, Toyota Landcruiser, Jeep, etc.). Invite them to use magazines and/or Internet sites to find a range of data, specifications and features. Then share in class, as presentations or in a discussion. You may wish to use the information to produce your own '4x4 Top Trumps'.

Name _____ Date _____

TREKKING ADVENTURE

Write an acrostic poem using the word TREKKING as the key word.

In your poem, try to show the feeling of adventure and excitement you would feel to be exploring a new landscape.

T _____

R _____

E _____

K _____

K _____

I _____

N _____

G _____

Introduction

- Ask the children to share their initial responses to this sound clip. What might be making this noise? Where, or when, have the pupils heard this before?

- Play the clip again. Establish that this is the sound of an electronic alarm clock. Is it similar to the children's own alarm clocks?

Discussion

- Do the children have alarm clocks of their own, or do their parents get them up? How easy or difficult do they find it? Share experiences and thoughts. Who is a lazy bones, a bed-bug or an early riser?

- What did people do before electronic alarm clocks? How did people wake up many years ago, before wind-up clocks were even invented?

Interaction

- In discussion groups, encourage the pupils to discuss how this sound makes them feel. Do they imagine they are in bed and must get up? Does it give them a jolt or 'wake-up call', even now?

- In pairs, invite the children to discuss what kind of alarm sound they would most like to wake up to. Share views in class, with individuals speaking on behalf of their partners.

Audio clip
ALARM CLOCK (05 secs)

WORD BANK

- Invite the children to write down some interesting words that describe the feelings that this sound clip evokes in them, e.g. *sleepy, drowsy, lazy, panic-stricken*. Share in class.

- Ask the pupils to make a list of onomatopoeic words that capture the sounds of different alarm clocks, rings and other wake-up calls (e.g. *beep, buzz, clang, ring, whirr, cock-a-doodle-doo*). These will be useful in the Wordsearch task below.

WRITING ACTIVITIES

Fiction

- **Sleepy poem:** Invite the children to write a descriptive poem all about sleeping in late, in which they capture the feelings of not wanting to get out of bed on a cold, dark morning in winter. They could begin with the sounds of the alarm clock ringing.

- **Similes and metaphors:** Discuss the terms 'night owl' and 'early bird'. Can the children think of some alternative similes or metaphors of their own to describe those who function best late in the evening or early in the morning? (E.g. *dawn worshippers/night soldiers; roosters/badgers*.)

Fiction

- **Humorous story:** Invite the children to plan and draft a short story in which the central character oversleeps and then faces a catalogue of humorous disasters as a result of having to rush. These might include: *burning the toast, wearing odd shoes, missing the bus, forgetting an umbrella*, etc.

- **Descriptive prose:** Invite the children to write two short pieces of prose: one to describe the warm, cosy feeling of snuggling in bed, the other to describe the harsh, bitter cold outside the bed, as they get up for school in winter. Encourage the use of similes and metaphors.

Non-Fiction

- **Personal writing (1):** Are they early birds or night owls? Do they like getting up in the morning or do they prefer to go to bed late and get up late? Encourage the children to share their thoughts and describe how much they like/dislike getting up in the morning.

- **Personal writing (2):** What song would the children most like to wake up to, and why? Encouragem to think for a few moments and then write down their choice, with reasons. Share these in class.

Non-Fiction

- **Annotated invention:** Invite the children to design a new type of wake-up-system – one that makes the breakfast, provides clothes to wear, does last minute homework, etc. Encourage them to annotate their design and write about its features and functions.

- **Advertising poster:** Invite the children to design and produce a poster that advertises their invention above. Consider together who the target audience may be (e.g. lazy teenagers, professionals in a rush, elderly people, etc.). Consider the impact of images and language used.

Extension

- **Story dialogue/playscript:** Invite the children to write a humorous dialogue between a teenager and his/her parent who is shouting upstairs to get them out of bed. What sort of threats can the parent issue? What excuses will the teenager give in order to stay in bed a bit longer?

Name _____ Date _____

WAKE-UP WORDSEARCH

Look again at the onomatopoeic words listed in your word bank.

Can you hide these in the Wordsearch grid below?

Write down the hidden words on the lines below, and then challenge your friends to find them.

Wake-up Words

_____ _____ _____

_____ _____ _____

_____ _____

_____

Introduction

- Ask the children to share their initial responses to this sound clip. What, or who might be making this noise?

- Play the clip again. Establish that this is the sound of a baby crying. But how young is the baby? Is this the sound of a tiny baby or a toddler? Share ideas.

Discussion

- Elicit the children's knowledge and experience of babies crying. Why do they cry? How should we react? Is it good for babies to cry sometimes? In what other ways do they communicate with others?

- What do the children think this particular baby is trying to say? Is he/she hungry perhaps? Or overtired? What do the children think? How can they tell?

Interaction

- In groups, discuss the idea of crying. Why do we cry? Is it something that only humans do? Do animals cry? What do animals do to attract attention and evoke sympathy? Share ideas.

- Consider together why we often make funny sounds ourselves when we talk to babies. Why do we 'coo-coo'? Is it to sound friendly, unthreatening, etc.? Encourage the children to share their thoughts and experiences of talking to babies.

Audio clip
BABY CRYING (31 secs)

WORD BANK

- Invite the children to try to capture the various noises that babies – and children generally – make in onomatopoeic words, e.g. *coo-coo, raagh, howl, giggle-giggle, gurgle,* etc. Share these in class.

- Ask the pupils to think about the kinds of words that young toddlers may pick up on and begin to say. What were the first words they said? Do they know? Make a list of possible high frequency words, e.g. *mummy, daddy, dummy, hello, bye-bye.* Share these in class. Which ones did they say first?

WRITING ACTIVITIES

Fiction

- **Humorous poem:** Invite the children to draft a short poem in which they record the world of language that a young child first experiences. Suggest that they write it from the baby's viewpoint, as it listens, incredulously, to grown up, intelligent people saying 'coo-coo' and 'ga-ga' in their face!

- **Similes and metaphors:** Consider how precious a baby is. Invite the children to come up with interesting similes and metaphors in sentences, to illustrate how much a baby is loved and valued, e.g. *like a jewel, an angel,* etc. Then repeat the exercise, this time to show how delicate a baby is.

Fiction

- **Science-fiction story:** Ask the children to plan and draft a short story in which an alien baby is found, abandoned in a remote part of a forest on Earth. Aliens landed and left the baby behind, either by accident or as an experiment to see if it (or we) would cope. What will happen next?

- **Descriptive prose:** Invite the children to put themselves in the mind of a young baby. Ask them to write a descriptive prose piece, in the first person, describing the baby's thoughts and reactions to the outside world/strangers' faces when it is first born.

Non-Fiction

- **Personal writing:** What sort of qualities do you think you need to be a successful babysitter, in a few years' time? Ask the children to respond to this question in a few sentences. Would they be interested in the job when they are old enough?

- **Earliest memory:** Ask the children to think carefully and then recount, briefly, their earliest memory as a child or toddler. Share these in class.

Non-Fiction

- **Instructional text:** Ask the children to design and produce an instructional text that offers basic advice on 'what to do with your new baby'. Discuss what the children might include, e.g. *feed regularly, change nappy when damp, remove wind by patting back, amuse by making funny faces!*

- **Recount:** Invite the children to imagine they have a new baby in the family, who has been in the house for a week. The children write a recount about the pleasures – and the frustrations – of the experience.

❗ Extension

- **Comic strip:** Invite the children to produce a page of comic strip about a new character, 'Superbabe', who is a 6-month-old baby with special powers. What challenge will Superbabe face in this week's adventure?

Name _____ Date _____

As you will know, to turn the word *baby* into a plural, you need to knock off the *y* and add *–ies*. The word *babys* looks wrong!

Can you remember how to change the following words into plurals? Be careful! Some are more difficult than others!

Singular	Plural
chimney	
diary	
journey	
leg	
penny	
donkey	
daisy	
glass	
box	
pie	
jelly	
appendix	
sheep	
goose	
cactus	
ox	
monkey	
tomato	
bus	

Mind's Eye/Writing   Year 6/BABY CRYING

Introduction

- Ask the children to share their initial responses to this sound clip. Where could it have been recorded? Do they recognise the sounds?

- Play the clip again. Establish that this is the sound of cicadas at night time, set in a jungle or rainforest of some kind.

Discussion

- Elicit the children's knowledge and experience of jungle settings. Have they seen jungles in films, books or actually visited them in real life? Can they describe the setting when they hear this sound?

- Establish what type of creature cicadas are. Compare them to crickets or grasshoppers in this country. What sort of noise do they make? Can anyone simulate the sound? Listen again together.

Interaction

- Ask the children to imagine they are trekking through this jungle setting. Ask for volunteers to sit in the 'hot seat' at the front and answer questions about their expedition. How do they feel? Where are they going? What sort of animals have they seen so far?

- In pairs, ask the pupils to make a list of other kinds of sound one might hear in this setting, over the sound of cicadas, e.g. *howls, roars, growls, screeches, rustling*. Share these idea in class.

Audio clip
CICADAS AT NIGHT (24 secs)

WORD BANK

- Encourage the children to write down some really interesting adjectives to describe the setting that is conjured up in their mind's eye when they hear this sound clip. Focus on the senses to stimulate good engagement with the setting. Share words – use thesauruses for richer, more vivid synonyms.

- Look at the word *cicadas* together. Ask them to come up with more examples of words with to c's in them, one soft, one hard: e.g. *cycle, practice, circle, circus, ceramic*. Use dictionaries.

WRITING ACTIVITIES

Fiction

- **Jungle poem:** Using the rich descriptive words in the word banks, the pupils draft a short poem about this jungle setting. Play the clip once again to stimulate their imagination. Consider rhyming schemes – you may wish to prescribe a particular pattern (e.g. *a,b,a,b* or *a,a,b,b*).

- **Descriptive prose:** Ask the children to write a paragraph or two of descriptive prose, using the first person, in which they are camping in a jungle setting at night time, to the sound of cicadas.

Non-Fiction

- **Glossary sentences:** Ask the pupils to consider the words with soft and hard c's in them, in their word banks, and then write a sentence for each one to show the meaning and context. Share these in class.

- **Personal writing:** What is the children's favourite jungle animal, and why? Ask them to write down their favourite and then provide several reasons for their choice. Share these in class. Is there a most popular animal? Why? Are some jungle animals more 'famous' than others? Why is this?

Fiction

- **Adventure story:** Ask the children to plan and draft a short story in which the central character finds themselves trekking through the jungle. Ask them to begin with the following sentence: *'Suddenly, through the steady sound of cicadas, there comes a spine-chilling screech and I am awake.'*

- **Character profile:** Invite the children to refer back to their favourite jungle animal, and then write a character profile for it, focusing on one particular animal in their mind – real or fictional. Encourage them to use personification to bring the animal closer to the reader's imagination.

Non-Fiction

- **Travel recount:** Ask the pupils to draft a short chronological text in which they recount a day in the jungle, during an imaginary expedition with friends or family. Encourage them to begin, and end, with the sound of cicadas. Share recounts in class. Which were more convincing, and why?

- **Non-chronological report:** Ask the children to choose a specific stretch of jungle/rainforest and research it, using Internet sites, atlases and encyclopaedias. Focus especially on the vast range of wildlife to be found in just a small area of jungle.

Extension

- **Persuasive writing:** Consider together the plight of the rainforests of the world: why are we losing so many at such a fast rate? What are the long-term effects of deforestation? Why should we all be aware of it? Ask the children to draft a persuasive speech, designed to make listeners realise how precious our rainforests are. Use websites (e.g. www.rainforestlive.org.uk) and encyclopaedias to find out more.

Name _____ Date _____

ENDANGERED SPECIES

Did you know that tropical rainforests cover 6% of the earth's surface, but they contain over 50% of all species?

Did you realise that we are losing 50 different species of animal or plant due to deforestation *every day*. That's two species per hour.

So which animals are next? Which species are endangered?

Find out more about the endangered animals of the rainforest. Write the name and some facts about each one in the spaces below.

Name of species	Fascinating facts
_____	_____ _____ _____ _____
_____	_____ _____ _____ _____
_____	_____ _____ _____ _____

Continue on a separate sheet if necessary.

© Rising Stars UK Ltd. 2007   Mind's Eye/Writing   Year 6/CICADAS AT NIGHT

Introduction

- Ask the children to share their initial responses to this sound clip. Brainstorm any initial key words and ideas on the board.

- Establish that this is the sound of a drum roll being played with sticks on a snare drum.

Discussion

- Elicit the children's knowledge and experience of forms of percussion. Do they know what a snare drum looks like? How is its sound produced?

- Consider together when and where one might hear a drum roll like the one in the sound clip. Record ideas on the board, e.g. *a magic show, a circus, a physical challenge of some sort*.

Interaction

- Discuss together what effect a drum roll has on an audience. Why is it used? (It builds suspense and excitement, etc.)

- In pairs, ask the children to come up with a theory as to the purpose and setting for this particular drum roll. Encourage them to build a picture of the scene, and then explain what happens next.

Audio clip
DRUM ROLL (20 secs)

WORD BANK

- Ask the children to focus on the rising and falling of the drum sound, in volume. Discuss the word *crescendo*. What does this mean? Can the children think of other musical terms (e.g. *forte, piano, staccato, arpeggio*)? Share them in class.

- Can the children think of interesting adjectives and abstract nouns to describe the excitement and tension which a drum roll conjures up – perhaps at a circus, magic show or theatre? Share ideas.

WRITING ACTIVITIES

Short task | Fiction

- **Poem:** Using the interesting words and phrases listed in their word banks, the children draft poems about a drum roll and a surprise that follows. Brainstorm ideas for settings and scenarios and then share opening lines.

- **Story beginning:** Discuss together how this sound clip might provide an idea for the opening scene for a story. Encourage the children to write the opening paragraph, and then share ideas.

Long task | Fiction

- **Short story:** Ask the children to draft a short story in which the central character finds themselves at a circus, magic show or pantomime, with a drum roll being played in anticipation of a big surprise, which then goes badly wrong...

- **Fictional recount:** Invite the children to imagine they are part of a circus act, which is about to go on stage in front of a live audience and perform some death-defying stunts or acrobatics. The drum roll plays, the crowd waits expectantly... how do they feel as they step out? What happens next? This is a chronological recount, in the first-person narrative.

Short task | Non-Fiction

- **Factual descriptions:** Give the children the names of five instruments each, and ask them to write a short description of each one, as it might appear in a dictionary or glossary.

- **Personal writing:** If the children could play any instrument at all, which would they take up, and why? (Perhaps they are already playing their dream instrument.) Encourage them to say what they like about it.

Long task | Non-Fiction

- **Personal writing:** Drum rolls are synonymous with great feats or challenges. What sort of feats would the children like to perform when they are older? What challenges would they like to take up, and why? Encourage the pupils to write down their thoughts, with reasons and explanations.

- **Information text:** Ask the children to choose a particular musical instrument, and then invite them to research information on it, using books, magazines and Internet sites. This can then be displayed as an information text, with annotated sketches and written text, providing interesting facts including: how it is played, history, sound type, etc.

Extension

- **Brainstorming ideas:** What other sorts of sounds would be just as exciting as a drum roll? How else could suspense and anticipation be built (e.g. *a bell ringing, stamping feet, vocal chants and rhythms*)? Ask the children to write down some ideas, and perhaps include sketches.

Name _____ Date _____

THE PERFECT SURPRISE!

Imagine that the drum roll in the sound clip is being played for you, at a party to celebrate your birthday.

The drum roll is played to tell you that the biggest surprise of all is about to be revealed. What would you most like it to be, and why?

Describe your dream surprise. It really could be anything!

_____

_____

_____

_____

_____

_____

_____

_____

_____

_____

_____

Introduction

- Ask the children to share their initial responses to this sound clip. Who, or what, do they think is making this noise?
- Play the clip again. Discuss the different sounds within the whole clip. Is this the sound of one animal, or several? How can we tell?

Discussion

- Establish that this is the sound of a gorilla. Play the clip again and then see if the children recognise any of its calls. Can anyone impersonate this gorilla? Encourage some volunteers to have a go!
- Elicit the children's knowledge and experience of gorillas. Where and when have they seen them? Can they describe the experience of seeing a real gorilla? Share memories and observations.

Interaction

- What do the children think this gorilla is saying in the clip? In pairs, invite the children to brainstorm some ideas. Then replay the clip and hear the translations!
- Invite the children to work in threes for this task. Encourage them to prepare a short role-play which comprises a dialogue between two gorillas, with a narrator (interpreter) interpreting for the audience.

Audio clip
GORILLA (14 secs)

WORD BANK

- Write the word *gorilla* on the board. Explain that it is one of those words that seems like it should have more double letters than it actually does. The same goes for *crocodile*. Can the pupils think of similar words that are often misspelt, either through insufficient or too many double letters? (E.g. *tomorrow, accommodation*).
- What would you call the sounds made in the clip? Encourage the children to write down these sounds in recognisable words, e.g. *snort, grunt, pant, breathe,* etc.

WRITING ACTIVITIES

Fiction

- **Acrostic poem:** Invite the children to draft an acrostic poem about the gorilla. Share these in class. Then set the children the task of writing more acrostics for other wild animals.
- **Alliterative phrases:** Revisit alliteration in class. Then challenge the children to think of alliterative phrases (noun and accompanying adjectives) for several wild animals. Encourage the children to select adjectives that are appropriate for each animal, e.g. *grouchy gorilla, slovenly sloth,* etc.

Non-Fiction

- **Factual account:** Play the clip once again. Ask the children to describe this clip in words, focusing on the detail of the types of noises, the frequency and the pitch. Discuss useful terms in class first, referring to the phrases used in the word banks to categorise different calls.
- **Personal writing:** If the children could learn to communicate with gorillas, what would they like to say? What things would they like to ask/explain/apologise for? Share notes in class.

Fiction

- **Playscript:** Invite the children to draft a playscript (or excerpt) in which a gorilla argues with a lion as to who should be crowned king of the jungle. What would be each animal's reasons? Share/perform in class.
- **Character description:** Using personification, similes and metaphors, the children write a short character description of the gorilla in the sound clip, drawing on what they can see in their mind's eye when the clip is replayed. Focus particularly on his/her character.

Non-Fiction

- **Letter:** Ask the children to draft a letter, written in role from the gorilla, to the world's people, pleading with them to pay attention to what is happening to his/her natural habitat, because of rapid deforestation. Encourage them to persuade readers to act now before gorillas become extinct forever.
- **Non-chronological report:** Invite the children to put together a non-chronological report on gorillas in the wild. Encourage them to focus their research on: habitat, species, diet, size and weight, and reasons why they are so threatened.

Extension

- Descriptive writing: Ask the children to put themselves in the mind of a gorilla who has just seen their very first human. What did they make of it? Challenge them to write a description of the strange creature they have just seen.

A VERY FIRST GLIMPSE

Think of a truly amazing wild animal, one that you would most like to see in real life.

Imagine that you are enjoying a safari with your family, in a place that is home to the wild animal you would most like to see.

After several hours of trekking, you finally get your very first glimpse of the animal. Describe this moment in detail. Think about the animal, the surrounding habitat and your own feelings at the time.

_____

_____

_____

_____

_____

_____

_____

_____

_____

_____

_____

_____

_____

_____

_____

_____

_____

Introduction

- Ask the children to share their initial responses to this sound clip. Who, or what, do they think is making these noises?

- Consider together where this may be set. Where might one hear such sounds, and why?

Discussion

- Establish that this is the sound of gunfire, of the kind one might see/hear in cowboy westerns. What might be happening in this scene? Share ideas and theories.

- Elicit the children's knowledge and experience of westerns. How can they be summed up? What sort of things happen in them? Share some common features of westerns.

Interaction

- In pairs, encourage the children to formulate proper theories about what is happening here, as they listen again to the clip and picture the scene. Share ideas in class.

- Invite volunteers to come to the 'hot seat' and answer questions in the role of one of the people in the scene from the sound clip. What is happening? Why are they shooting? What happens next?

Audio clip
GUNFIRE (32 secs)

WORD BANK

- Encourage the children to record down the language of westerns – some interesting words and phrases that are common to such films and settings, e.g. *posse, sheriff, cut them off at the pass, jailhouse, railroad,* etc.

- Can the children think of some interesting onomatopoeic words that are associated with gunfire and explosions? (E.g. *whiz, bang, crack, split,* etc.)

WRITING ACTIVITIES

Fiction

- **Cowboy poem:** Ask the children to plan and draft a poem all about life as a cowboy/cowgirl, driving cattle across the plains of America. Consider together the life of a cowboy – how they make their living, what their daily life is like, etc. Focus too on the spectacular scenery all around.

- **Story beginning:** Invite the children to write the opening paragraph to a story, in which the sounds in the clip make up the opening scene. Where is it set? Why are the people firing? What happens next?

Fiction

- **Film storyboard:** Invite the children to design and produce a storyboard from a western film, in which this scene is featured. What happens to create this gun battle? What will happen next? How many characters are involved? Where are they fighting, and why? The pupils present their ideas.

- **Character description:** Invite the children to choose one of the 'cowboys or cowgirls' which they can picture as they hear this sound clip, and to write a character profile for this person, focusing on their appearance, skills, occupation and personality. They could include a sketched portrait of their imaginary character.

Non-Fiction

- **Compound words:** Revise compound words, beginning with 'cowboy'. Encourage the children to make a list of new compound words and then share them in class.

- **Personal writing:** If the children were given the opportunity to work as a cattle rancher, would they go for it? Is it the sort of life they would like? Encourage them to explain their thoughts and offer reasons in support.

Non-Fiction

- **Discussion text:** Should people be allowed to keep guns for private use, even with a licence? Should guns only be used by professional marksmen? What are the arguments on either side? Discuss/debate this in class and then encourage the children to write it up as a discursive text, profiling views for and against guns used for field sports.

- **Debate speech:** Ask the children to draft a speech either proposing or opposing the following motion: *All police officers in this country should be issued with a firearm.* Discuss the inherent issues and then challenge them to write a speech, which can then be read out in a proper class debate.

Extension

- **Descriptive writing:** Ask the children to draft a page of descriptive prose, describing the scene which they imagine when they listen to the sound clip. Encourage them to focus on the sounds, sights, smells and atmosphere of the location, and descriptions of the characters involved.

Name _____ Date _____

STORY PLAN

Read your story beginning from the short fiction task.

Now see if you can write a plan for the whole story, so that you can continue writing it.

You will need to think about:

- **Characters**

_____

_____

_____

- **Setting(s)**

_____

_____

_____

- **Story plot**

_____

_____

_____

_____

_____

_____

_____

Introduction

- Ask the children to share their initial responses to this sound clip. Where and when have they heard this sound before? What could be making it?

- Establish that this is the sound of a police siren in full flow. Play the clip once again and encourage the children to picture the scene. What can they see?

Discussion

- Elicit the children's knowledge and experience of emergency vehicles hurtling through traffic. What should other drivers do?

- Consider together where this particular police car (or van) may be going. Share ideas and theories.

Interaction

- Invite volunteers to sit in the 'hot seat' and answer questions from the class in the role of the driver of this police vehicle. Where are they going, and why? How fast are they driving?

- What other kinds of siren or alarm do we hear in cities and towns (e.g. *burglar alarm, car alarm, fire engine, ambulance*)? Working in pairs, the children write down some ideas and then feed back to the class.

Audio clip
POLICE SIREN (08 secs)

WORD BANK

- Ask the children to try to put this alarm sound into words – either established ones or invented words and phrases. Share these in class. What other onomatopoeic words can describe alarm sounds?

- Encourage the children to write down some adjectives or abstract nouns that capture how they feel when they first hear this sound, e.g. *fearful, curious, worried, helpful, interested, alarmed*. Share these in class.

WRITING ACTIVITIES

Short task — Fiction

- **Descriptive writing:** Ask the children to describe the scene which they picture, as the sound clip is played. Encourage them to think about: location, police vehicle, other cars, reaction of motorists and pedestrians.

- **Sounds poem:** Ask the children to think about the different sounds one might hear on a typical day in the city. Record these in a poem, packed full of onomatopoeic words and rhythms. Begin by writing the first stanza together in class.

Long task — Fiction

- **Story scene:** Invite the children to plan and draft a short scene from an imaginary story, in which the central character participates in a high-speed chase, in the role of a police officer. Who are they chasing, and why? What happens once the chase ends?

- **Radio dialogue:** Discuss together the walkie talkie systems that the police may use, while out and about, so they can contact headquarters. Ask the pupils to draft a short dialogue or playscript which might be heard over the airwaves. Where is the police officer going, and why? How will HQ assist?

Short task — Non-Fiction

- **List of ideas:** If the siren wasn't used, how else could police officers attract the attention of passers by and clear a passage through traffic? What do the children think? Ask them to note down some ideas and then share them in class (e.g. *horn, shouting, banging a drum, ringing a bell,* etc.).

- **Annotated design:** What will police cars look like in the year 2107? Ask the children to sketch a design and then annotate it to show the different features and functions.

Long task — Non-Fiction

- **Chronological report:** Ask the children to conduct some research into what a 'day in the life of a police officer' may be like in our towns or cities. Using the Internet, books and magazines, the pupils piece together a typical day of duties, including written text, times, diagrams, maps and pictures.

- **Personal writing:** Would the children like to become a police officer when they leave school? What are their views on it? Encourage them to share these in a short written text, and then within a class discussion on careers in the police force.

Extension

- **Person specification:** Ask the children to consider the kinds of qualities and skills one might need to become a good police officer today. Then write these down in the form of a person specification, of the kind that often accompanies a job description. Discuss how this might be laid out in class.

Name _____ Date _____

NEW RECRUITS NEEDED!

Design an advertisement that may appear in a local newspaper, for new recruits to join the police force.

Try to make the advertisement appealing to readers, by describing police work, the skills needed and the opportunities to make a difference to people's lives. Why should people join the force today?

Introduction

- Ask the children to share their initial responses to this sound clip. Who or what might be making this noise?
- Consider together where this may have been recorded. How can we tell? Have the children heard anything like this before? Is water involved?

Discussion

- Establish that this is the sound of a scuba diver, underwater. Play the clip again and identify the breathing in at the beginning and then the breathing out, which causes the bubbles you can hear.
- Elicit the children's knowledge and experience of being underwater. What does it feel like? Does anyone have any interesting stories of diving while on holiday, or in a pool?

Interaction

- Working in pairs, the children note down some interesting theories about where this person could be located, as they picture the setting and action. Share ideas in class.
- Working in pairs or small discussion groups, invite the children to consider what other interesting things this could be, if it were not a scuba diver, e.g. *an alien, a giant robotic fish*. Share these ideas in class.

Audio clip
SCUBA DIVING (05 secs)

WORD BANK

- Ask the pupils to write down some verbs that we might associate with water – onomatopoeic or otherwise, e.g. *gurgling, rippling, splashing, diving, bubbling*, etc. Share in class.
- Write down the word *dive* and remind the children of how to put *–ing* on the end by knocking off the letter *–e* first. How many other verbs can they think of that require the same change, in two minutes? Share words and check spelling.

WRITING ACTIVITIES

Fiction

- **Watery poem:** Invite the children to draft a poem with a watery theme, using the verbs associated with water, listed in their word banks. Share opening lines in class. You may wish to focus particularly on diving as a subject.
- **Descriptive sentences:** For each of the watery verbs above, encourage the children to write a short, descriptive sentence, to illustrate its meaning and context. Share any particularly interesting sentences in class. Then explore any other meanings and contexts for the verbs (e.g. *splashing out on something, bubbling with rage*).

Non-Fiction

- **Postcard:** Invite the children to imagine they are enjoying a scuba diving holiday abroad. Ask them to write a postcard to their friends back home, telling what they have got up to and how it feels to be looking for natural treasures beneath the waves.
- **Annotated design:** What will diving equipment look like in many years' time? Encourage the children to design their own personal diving outfits of the future. What kind of features will the suit have? (E.g. *built in mini-propeller, sound system, able to withstand higher pressure*, etc.)

Fiction

- **Adventure story:** Discuss what the children know of the legend of Atlantis. Ask the pupils to plan and draft an adventure story set underwater, where a group of divers discover a lost city, with treasure and amazing architecture, unseen for thousands of years.
- **Playscript:** Invite the children to draft a short dialogue/playscript between two divers, on their way out to sea to go diving. One is an experienced diver; the other has never dived before and feels very nervous. Perform, and appraise, the scripts in class.

Non-Fiction

- **Non-chronological report:** Ask the children to design and produce a non-chronological report on scuba diving, drawing information from a range of sources, including websites, encyclopaedias, books and magazines. Share texts in class and discuss the use of text, images and annotations.
- **Persuasive writing:** Ask the children to draft an excerpt from a fictional holiday brochure, in which scuba diving holidays are advertised off the coast of some exotic islands. What will the tourists be able to see beneath the waves? Why should they make the trip? Why will it be a holiday to remember?

Extension

- **Journalistic text:** Ask the children to draft a newspaper article which reports the story of a local diver who makes the most remarkable find underwater. Discuss what the find might be (e.g. *treasure, ship, new kind of fish*). Encourage the children to include eyewitness accounts and expert opinions about the find.

Name _____ Date _____

EXTREME SPORTS

Would you like to go scuba diving? What other extreme sports would you most like to do, and why?

Write down the name of the extreme sport below, and then give some reasons why you would like to try it out. Who knows, perhaps one day you will!

My favourite extreme sport would be:

_____

I would like to try this sport because:

_____

_____

_____

_____

_____

_____

_____

_____

_____

Introduction

- Ask the children to share their initial responses to this sound clip. Who or what might be making this noise? Where is it set?

- Establish that this is the sound of spectators at a sports event. What kind of sport is being played? How can we tell? (E.g. the sound of the umpire's voice suggests tennis.)

Discussion

- Confirm that this is the sound recording of a tennis match being played, and the voice you hear is the umpire. Play the clip again and recognise the different sounds and features.

- Elicit the children's knowledge and experience of tennis tournaments, e.g. Wimbledon. Has anyone seen Wimbledon on television, or visited it in person? What was it like?

Interaction

- Working in pairs, the children consider what has just happened in the sound clip, and formulate a theory (e.g. a winning point has been played, the players have just come out). Share in class.

- Working in groups, the children prepare a short piece of 'radio drama' in which they perform a sequence of sounds to simulate a tennis match in full flow. Perform and share responses.

Audio clip
TENNIS CROWD (13 secs)

WORD BANK

- Consider together the language of tennis scoring. Invite volunteers to see if they can write out the correct terms accurately on the board (i.e. *love, fifteen, thirty, forty, deuce, advantage, game*). Consider what these mean in a tennis context, especially the terms 'love' and 'deuce'.

- Consider the word *crowd*. Revisit/introduce collective nouns. Ask the children to make a list of other collective nouns and then share them in a plenary. Check spelling, meaning and context each time.

WRITING ACTIVITIES

Fiction

- **Nouns poem:** Invite the children to draft a short poem which includes some of the collective nouns listed in the word bank. Draft the opening stanza in class. Look at ways of incorporating rhyme too.

- **Tennis poem:** Consider together the model of a tennis game, the ball switching back and forth, left to right, like a metronome. How can this be reflected in poetry? Write a class poem about tennis which uses alternating rhyme and rhythm patterns to reflect the movement of the ball.

Non-Fiction

- **Introductions:** Ask the children to imagine they are the commentator for this match. He/she introduces the players as they step out onto the court. What might he/she say? The children write a few lines of introduction for each player. (E.g. '*Three times Wimbledon champion, world number one seed...*', etc).

- **Note-making:** Encourage the children to make some notes on the skills and qualities they think are needed to become a world-class tennis player. Discuss these in class.

Fiction

- **Sporting story:** Invite the children to plan and draft a short story in which the central character works hard at becoming the best in their field – and then finally achieves world class success. How does the character feel when they finally reach the top?

- **Playscript:** Encourage the pupils to write a short playscript between two tennis players and an umpire. During a match, the umpire makes a call which one of the players strongly disputes. How will they solve the dispute? What will happen? Perform the scripts in class.

Non-Fiction

- **Personal writing:** If the children could become world class standard in any sport, which would they choose, and why? Invite the children to read out their work and then answer questions about their choice. Are there one or two favourite sports in the class? Why is this?

- **Journalistic text:** Invite the children to write a newspaper article about an exciting new tennis school that is opening in their town. Funded by a world famous player, it will coach young talent at weekends and after school. Include the comments of locals, including some who are objecting.

Extension

- **Class debate:** Discuss the above proposal for the tennis school, and focus on why some locals may object (e.g. *would rather it was a soccer school/will be unsightly for neighbours, more traffic*, etc). Then ask the pupils to write speeches for or against the plan. Hold a debate or 'planning meeting' to hear the views of the local community.

Name _____ Date _____

A SPORTING LEGEND

Who is your sporting hero? Is there someone whom you admire, whose career you have keenly followed?

Why do you admire this person? Would you like to be like them? Will you follow in their footsteps?

Write down the name of your sporting hero and then explain why you admire this person. Refer to their qualities, skills and achievements.

My sporting hero is:

_____

I admire this person because:

_____

_____

_____

_____

_____

_____

_____

_____

_____

_____

Introduction

- Ask the children to share their initial responses to this sound clip. Who or what might be making this noise?

- Take suggestions from the class about where this sound may have been recorded. Have they heard a similar sound before? Where?

Discussion

- Establish that this is the sound of a tap dripping. Explain how many people find this kind of repetitive noise irritating. Why is this? How do the children react to it? Share emotional responses.

- What other kinds of repeated sounds can one hear around a house? Share ideas (e.g. *wind blowing a gate, pipes clanking, sink gurgling, mice or rats scratching, birds scurrying*).

Interaction

- Ask the children to listen again to the image and try to picture the location. Then invite volunteers to describe their personal picture to the class so they can share in it. Do some have similar images in their heads?

- Invite the children to prepare a dialogue between a couple. One is nagging the other to fix the dripping tap 'like they said they would weeks ago'. The noise irritates one, but not the other person!

Audio clip
WATER DRIPPING (39 secs)

WORD BANK

- Ask the children to invent their own onomatopoeic words for the kind of repeated sounds discussed previously, e.g. *gluggle gluggle, tink, tink, tink*.

- Invite the children to write down some interesting adjectives to describe how a listener may feel after a few minutes of a dripping tap, or a clanking pipe, e.g. *frustrated, irritated, anxious, unsettled*.

WRITING ACTIVITIES

Fiction
Short task

- **Descriptive phrases:** For each of the irritating sounds listed in the earlier discussion, ask the children to write a sentence or phrase which contains adjectives, similes or metaphors to reflect how irritating the noise can become, e.g. *clanking like a ships' bell, the constant dripping stabs like a sword*.

- **Descriptive writing:** Invite the children to draft a short piece of descriptive prose in which they describe an old, derelict house, which echoes to the solitary sound of a tap dripping. There is silence throughout, as the drips ring around the empty rooms, until something else stirs…

Non-Fiction
Short task

- **Personal writing:** Ask the children to think carefully about the kinds of sounds that they regularly hear at home – they may be sounds that have become unnoticed now, they are so regular. Share these in class (e.g. *clock ticking, fridge humming, boiler firing up*).

- **Advertisement:** Ask the children to draft a short newspaper advertisement offering the services of a plumber. How can the greatest impact be made, and the most information be given, in a few words? You may wish to place a word limit on it (e.g. 25 words).

Fiction
Long task

- **Ghost story:** Ask the children to refer back to the piece of prose which describes the empty house. Invite them to continue this as a ghost story, in which the central character enters the house for a dare, but soon find that the dripping tap is not the only sound that haunts them…

- **Sounds poem:** Invite the children to draft a substantial poem in which various repeating, irritating sounds are mentioned. The poem could be written in the first person, from the viewpoint of someone who has to endure these sounds each day in the 'house that talks'.

Non-Fiction
Long task

- **Letter:** Invite the children to draft a letter of complaint from a tenant to a landlord, asking him/her to fix a dripping pipe that has been slowly leaking for weeks. The noise is driving them mad! Discuss ways of writing the letter so as to achieve the best response.

- **Non-chronological text:** They say you'll never go hungry as a plumber, but what do plumbers actually do? Encourage the children to find out more, by reading encyclopaedias, DIY books, magazines and Internet sites. Share feedback and ask the children to put together a two-page spread, with pictures, diagrams, annotations and written text.

❗ Extension

- **Short story:** Ask the children to plan and draft a story in which a leaking pipe slowly leads to a flood in a house, while the owners are away. When they return, they are horrified to find the carpet under two inches of water! And where is the cat? Explore scenarios and possible plot lines.

'STOP THAT RACKET!'

What kind of noise is frustrating for *you*? What can't you bear to listen to? Nails on a blackboard, perhaps? Or the constant throb of loud music in the back of a car?

Describe the kind of sound you would not be able to listen to for very long! Then explain how this sound makes you *feel*.

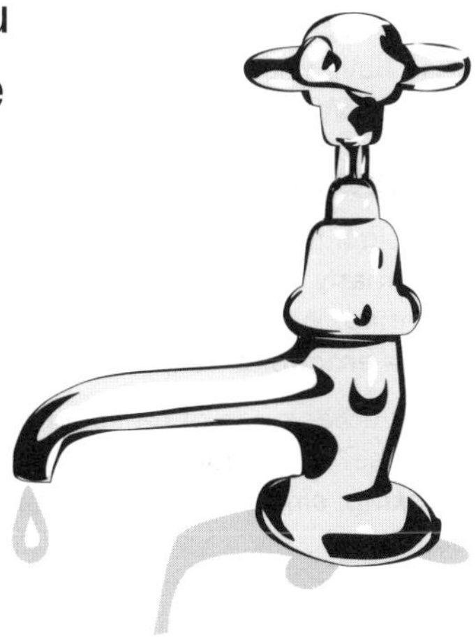

_____

_____

_____

_____

_____

_____

_____

_____

_____

_____

_____

_____

OVERVIEW OF TEXT TYPES AND CROSS-CURRICULAR LINKS TO SUPPORT PLANNING
Planning blocks taken from *Primary Framework: Year 6 Literacy Planning*

Mind's Eye Unit	Literacy planning blocks and text types at a glance			Opportunities for cross-curricular links
	Narrative	**Non-fiction**	**Poetry**	
ABSEILING	Adventure story Film scenes	Journalistic text Information text	Riddle	Art and Design Science
BALL AND CHAIN	Descriptive writing Fantasy story	Diary Debate speech	Descriptive poem	History PSHE
CANDLE	Historical story Mystery story	Chronological report Explanation text	Acrostic poem	Science History
COASTLINE	Sea adventure Mystery story	Safety instructions poster Advertisement	Descriptive poem	Geography Art and Design
COMPASS	Character study Adventure story	Written directions Recount; Chronological report	Geographical poem Descriptive poem	Geography History
DERELICT BUILDING	Mystery story Descriptive prose	Formal letter Journalistic text	Long descriptive poem	Design and Technology
DOORS	Science-fiction story Descriptive prose	Explanation text Instructions text	Riddle	PSHE Science; Design and Technology
HANDS	Adventure story Descriptive prose	Persuasive flier Explanation text	Hands poem	ICT; Science Art and Design
HIPPOS	Animal adventure Character studies	Factfile cards Informative presentation	Acrostic poem	Geography ICT
HOUSES OF PARLIAMENT	Historical story/comic strip Adventure story	Journalistic text Debate speech	Sounds poem	PSHE/Citizenship History
JET FIGHTER	Adventure story Science-fiction story	Discussion text Information text	Descriptive poem	Design and Technology
KEYHOLE	Mystery story Descriptive prose	Radio advertisement Captions	Riddle	Art and Design PSHE
MISTY HARBOUR	Ghost story Adventure story	Journalistic text; Glossary Weather report	Figurative poem	Geography; ICT Science
NEPALESE TOWN	Fantasy story Fictional recount	Discussion text Diary extract; Informal letter	Haiku	Geography
OLD PHOTOGRAPH	Historical story Science-fiction story	Dictionary/reference text Explanation text	Acrostic poem	History; Design and Technology ICT
RIDERS	Song lyrics Seaside adventure	Instruction text Discussion text	Onomatopoeic poem	Geography Music
ROBOWOMAN	Science-fiction story Robot narrative	Journalistic text Discussion text	Robot poem	Design and Technology; ICT Science
ROLLER COASTER	Science-fiction story Descriptive prose	Radio transcript Persuasive slogans	Shape poem	Art and Design ICT
ROOFTOPS	Fantasy story Science-fiction story	Annotated design Personal writing	Figurative poem Riddle	RE; Design and Technology Art and Design
TREKKING	Film storyboard Adventure story	Persuasive brochure Discussion text	Trekking poem	Geography Design and Technology

Mind's Eye Unit	Literacy planning blocks and text types at a glance			Opportunities for cross-curricular links
	Narrative	**Non-fiction**	**Poetry**	
ALARM CLOCK	Humorous story Descriptive writing	Instructions Discussion text	Descriptive poem	Design and Technology PSHE
BABY CRYING	Science-fiction story Descriptive prose	Instructional text Personal writing; Recount	Humorous poem	Science PSHE
CICADAS AT NIGHT	Adventure story Character profile	Letter Annotated design	Descriptive poem	Geography Citizenship
DRUM ROLL	Short story Fictional recount	Personal writing Information text	Descriptive poem	Music PSHE
GORILLA	Descriptive writing Playscript	Letter Non-chronological report	Acrostic poem	Geography PSHE/Citizenship
GUNFIRE	Film storyboard Character description	Personal writing Discussion text	Cowboy poem	History Geography
POLICE SIREN	Story scene Radio dialogue	Chronological report Newspaper advertisement	Onomatopoeia poem	PSHE/Citizenship
SCUBA DIVING	Playscript Adventure story	Chronological report Persuasive writing	Water poem	Geography
TENNIS CROWD	Playscript Sports story	Journalistic text Note-making	Rhythmic poem Nouns poem	PE PSHE
WATER DRIPPING	Ghost story Descriptive writing	Non-chronological report Letter	Sound poem	Music Science